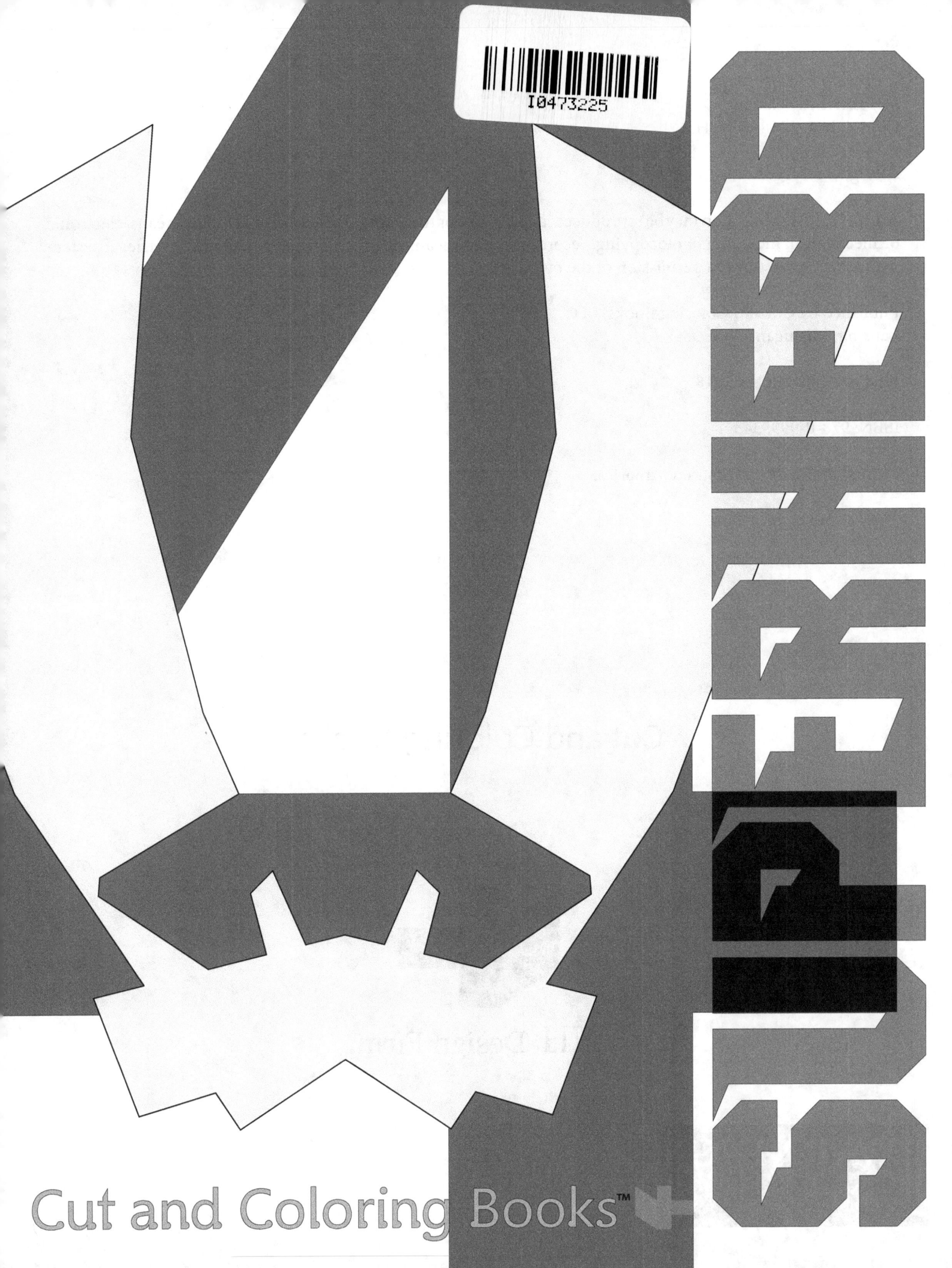

SUPERHEROS

Cut and Coloring Books™

Published by Cut and Coloring Books, LLC.
Lansing, Michigan

First edition October 2018

ISBN: 978-0-9995343-4-2

Printed in the United States of America.

Cut and Coloring Books.

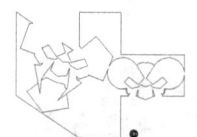

is a complete partner with

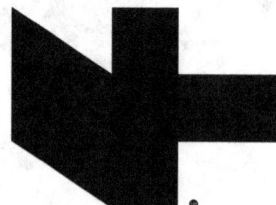

NH Design Firm.

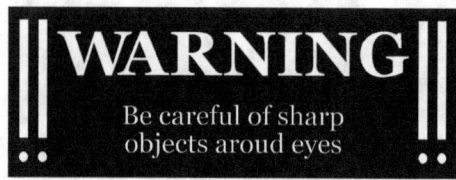

WARNING

Be careful of sharp
objects aroud eyes

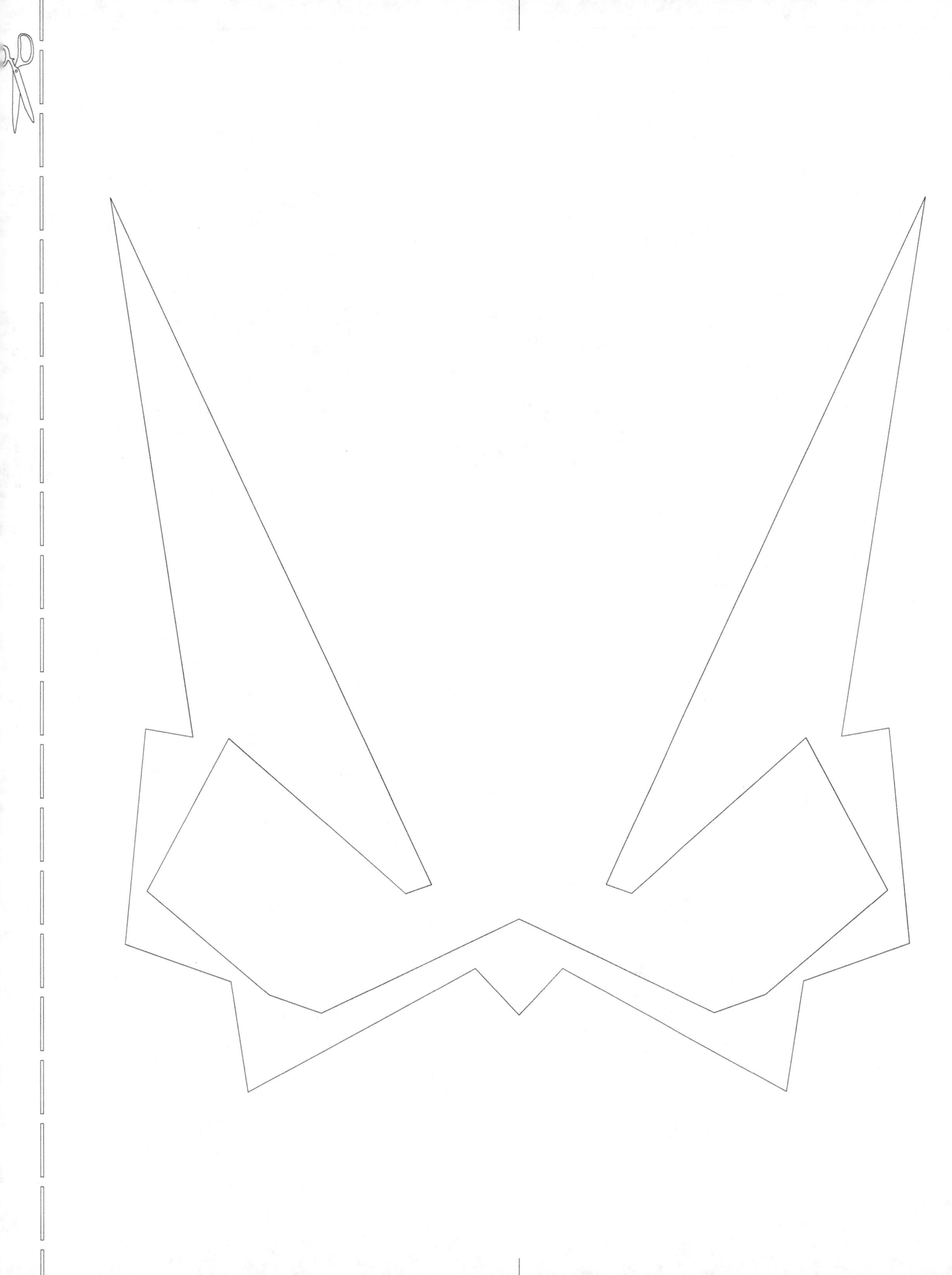

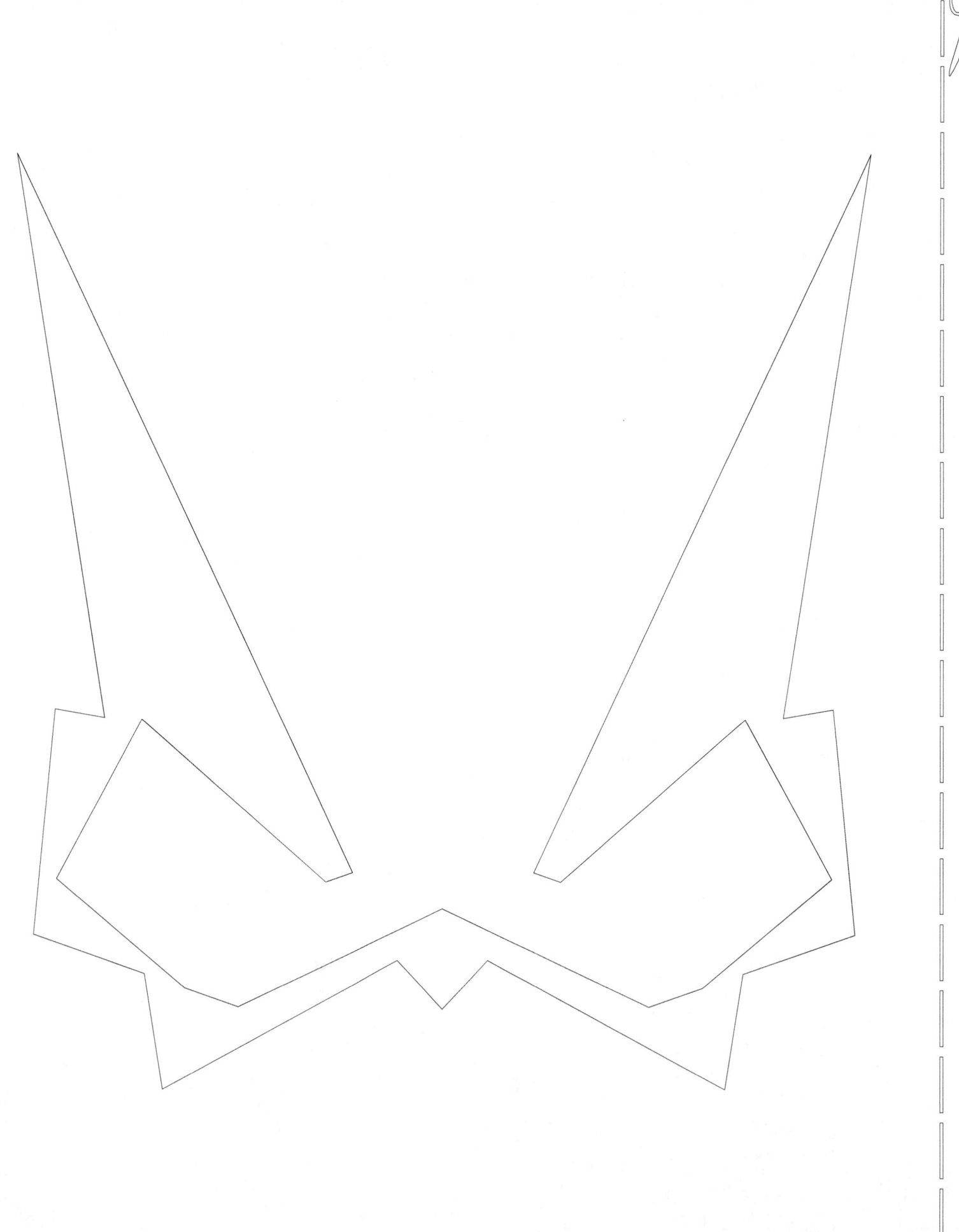

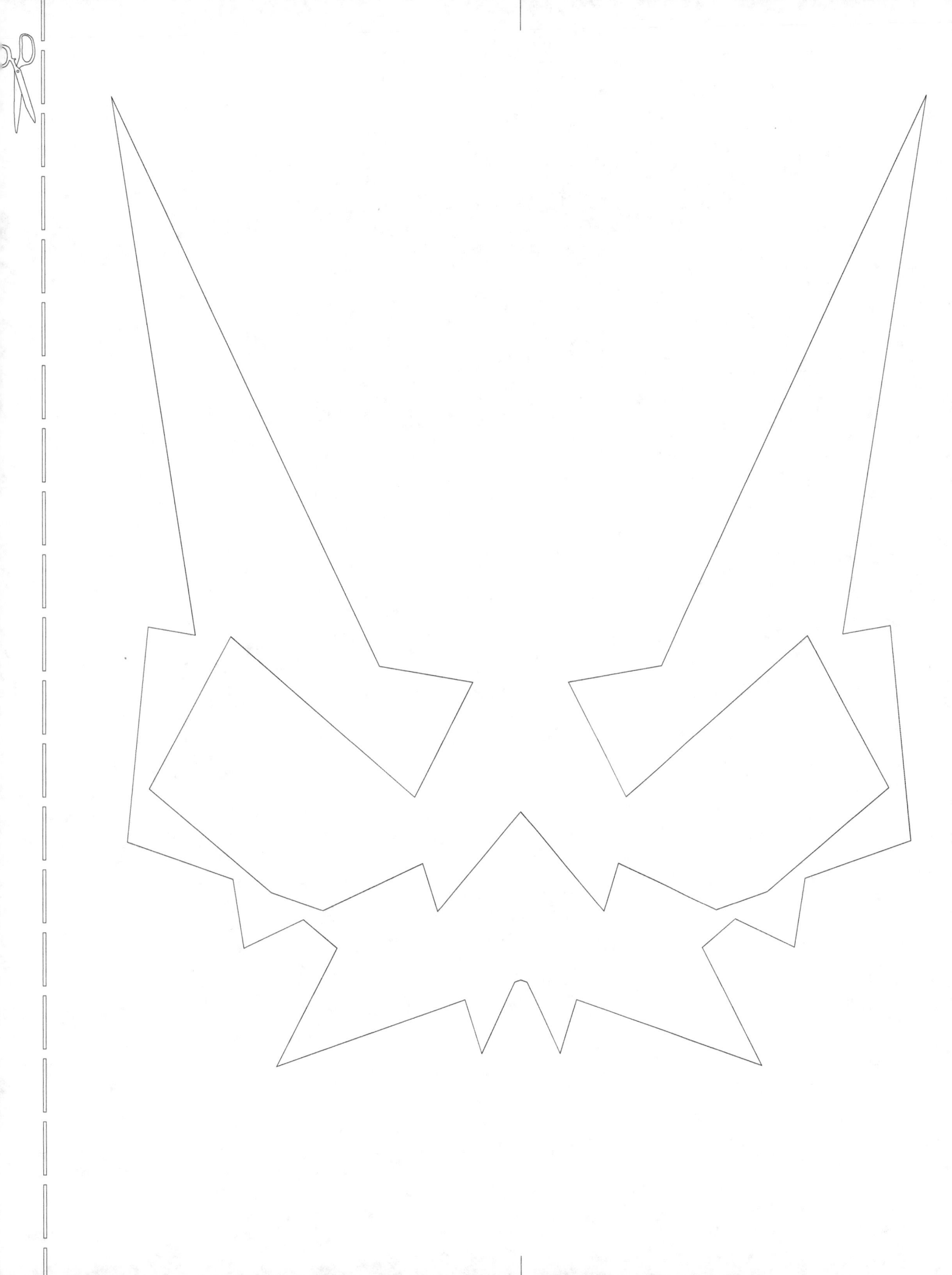

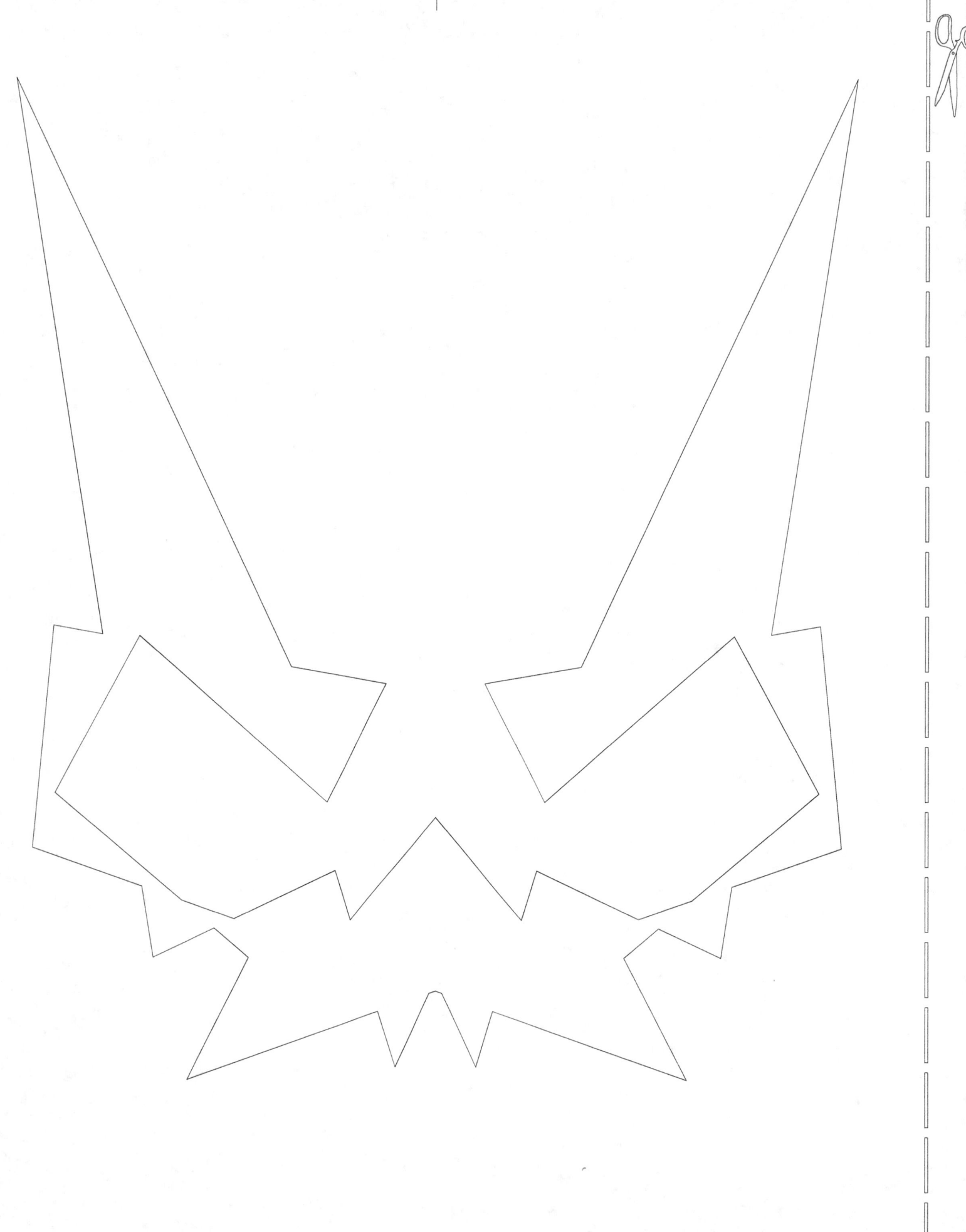

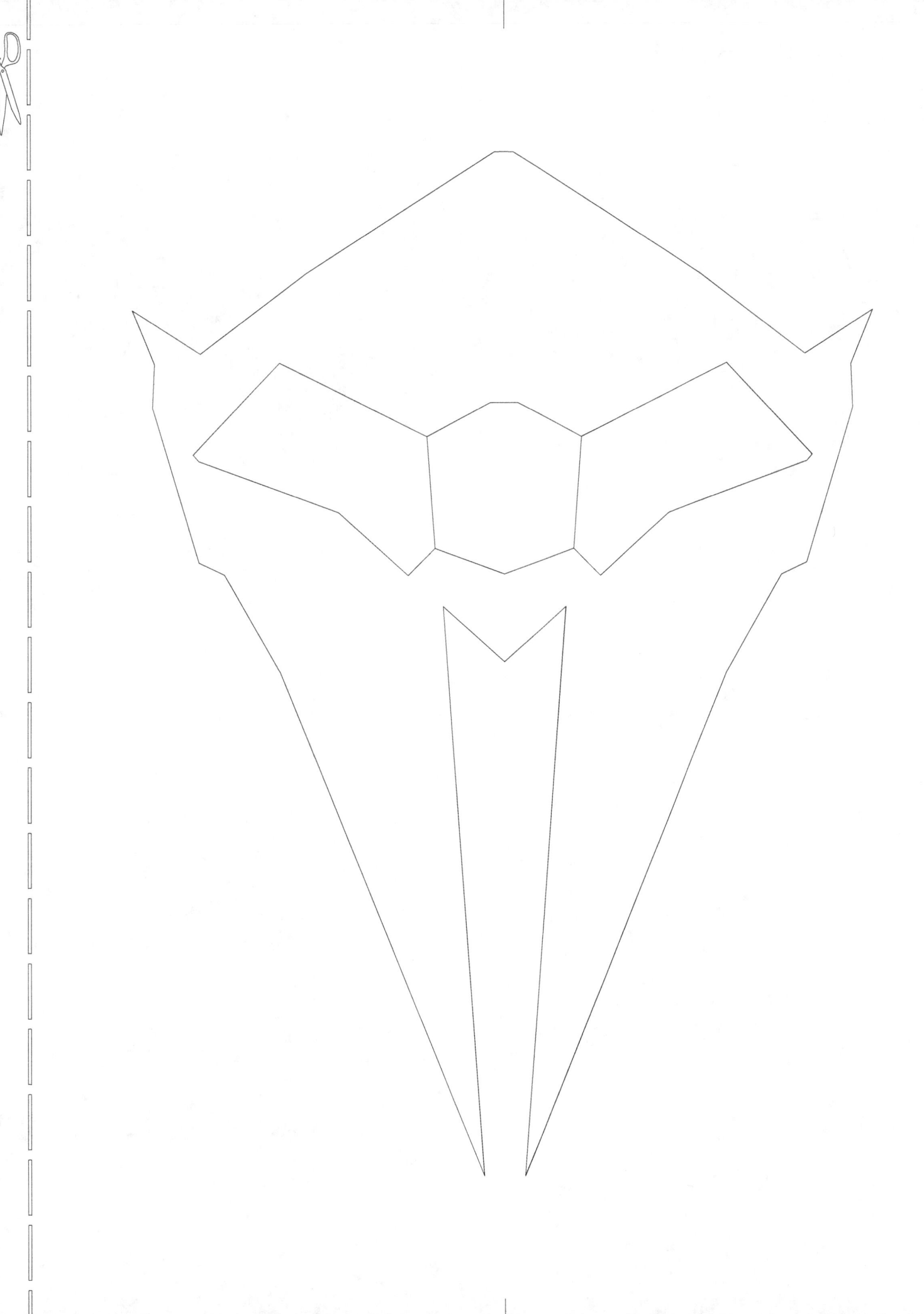

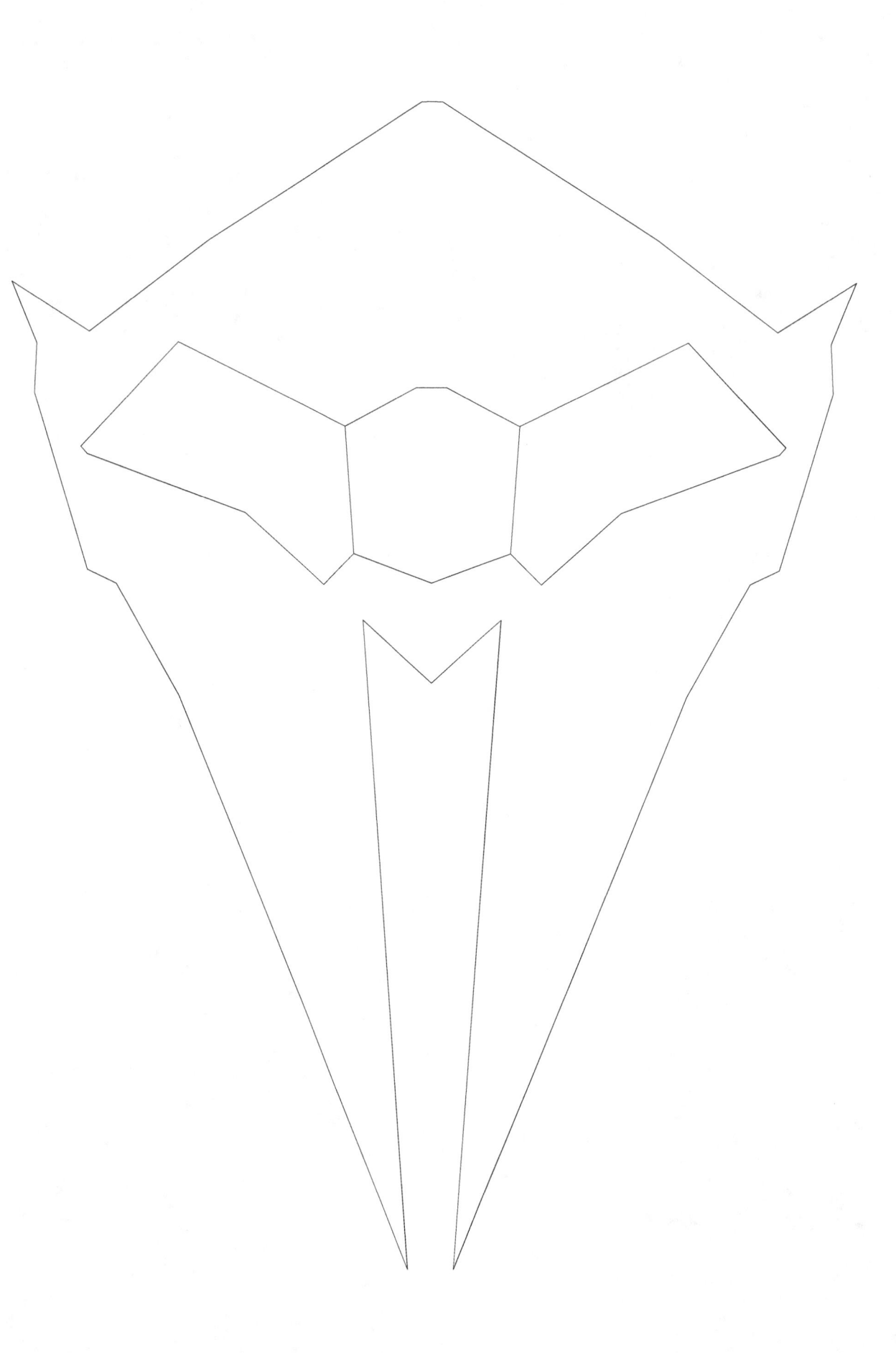

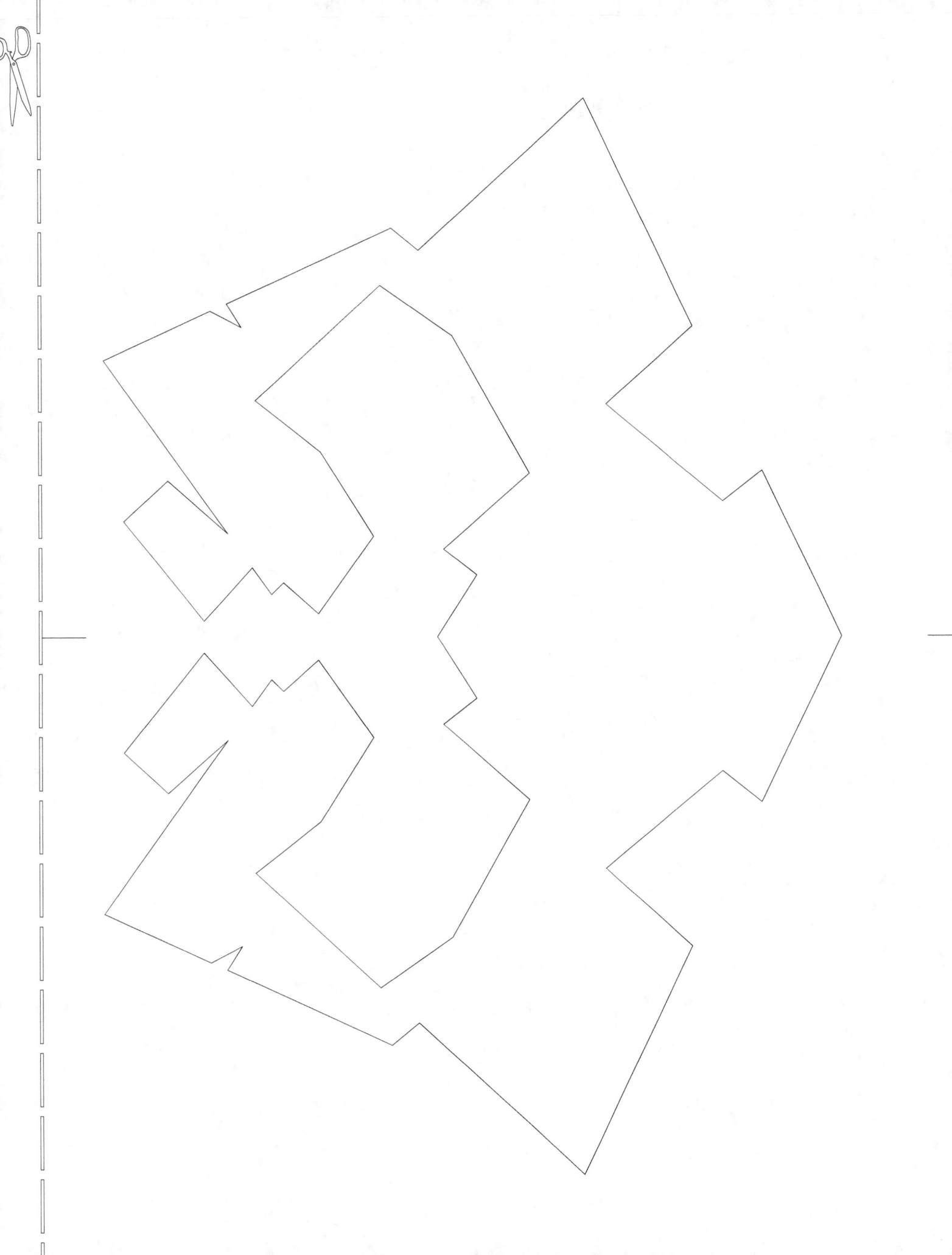

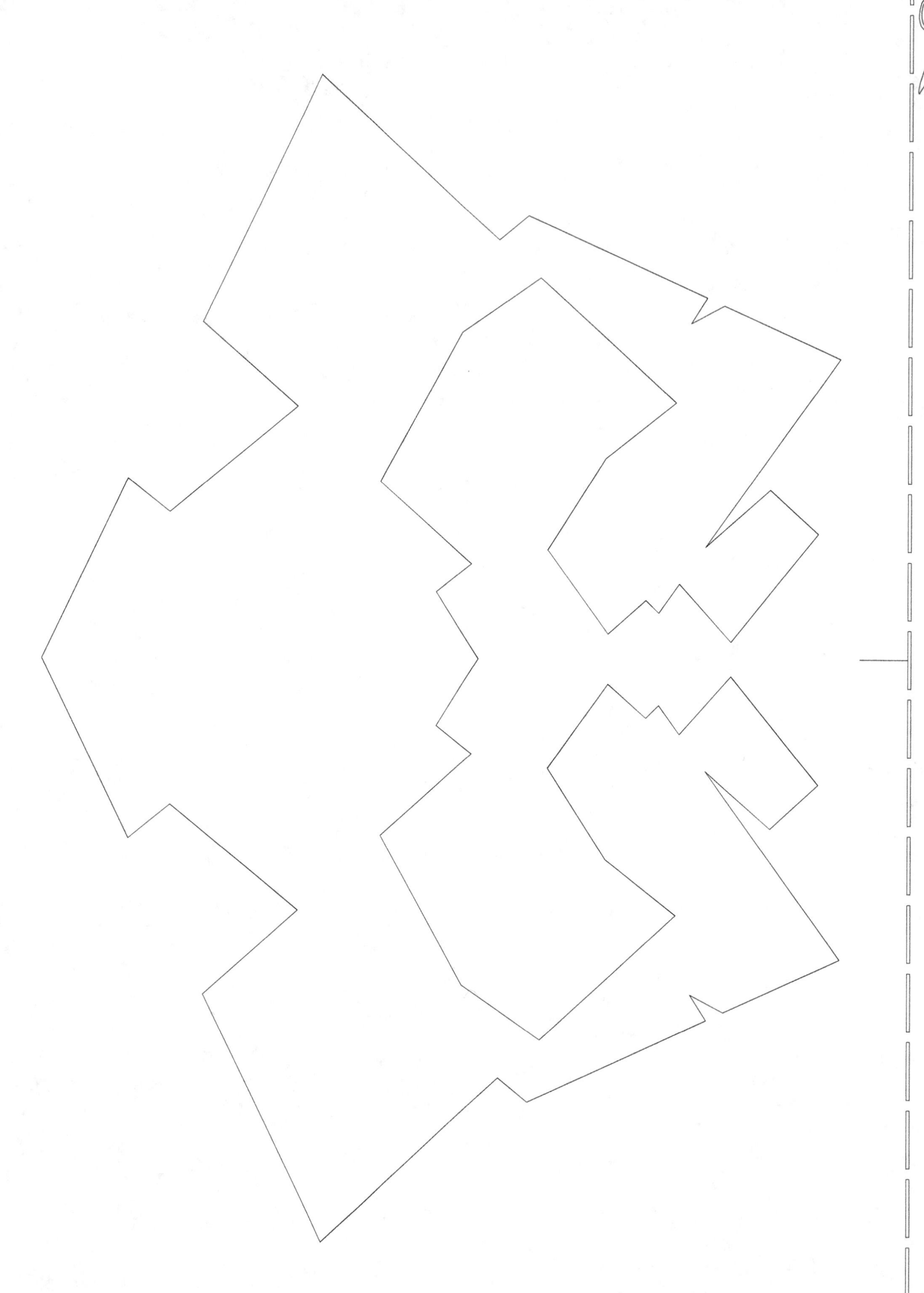

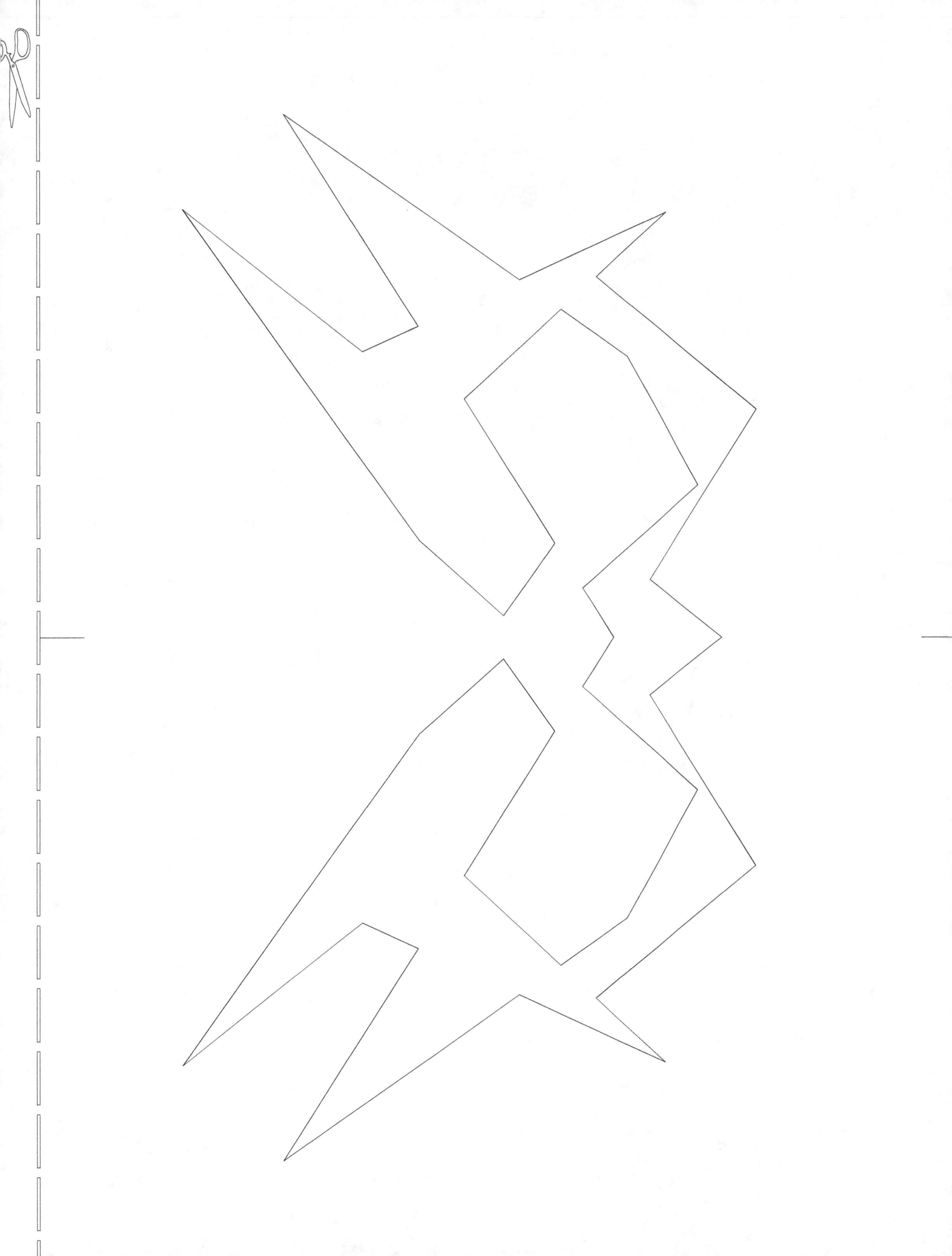

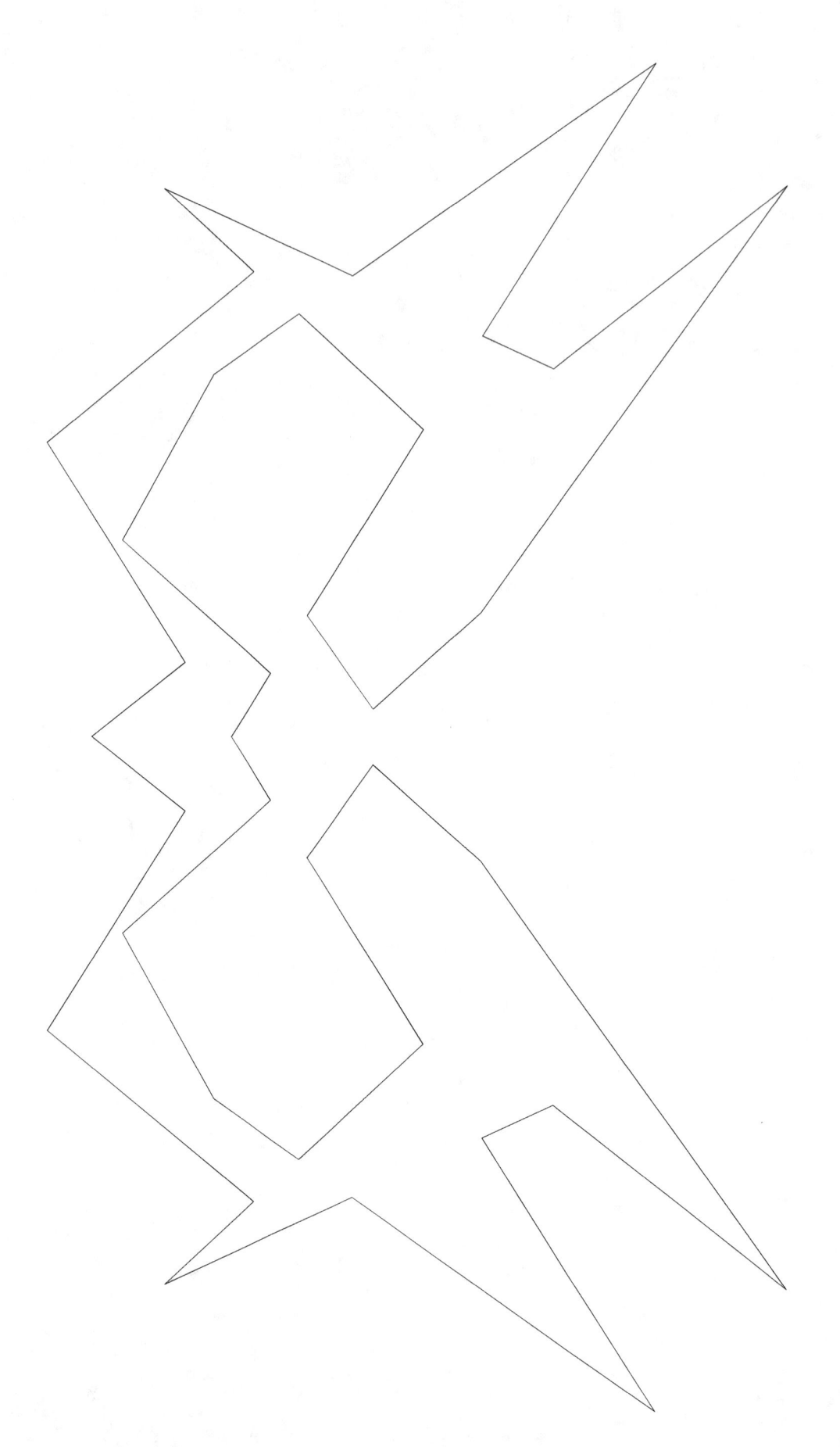

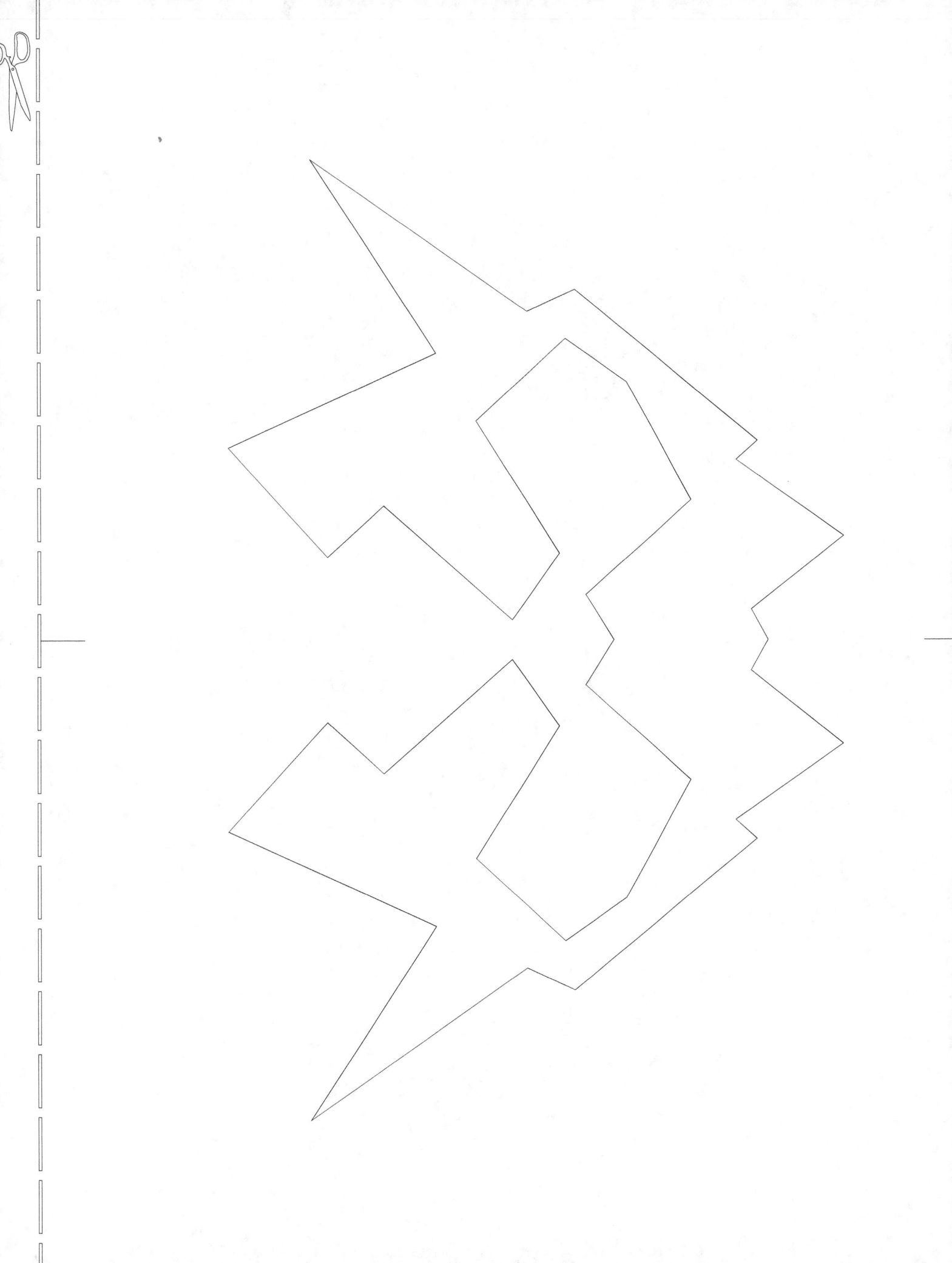

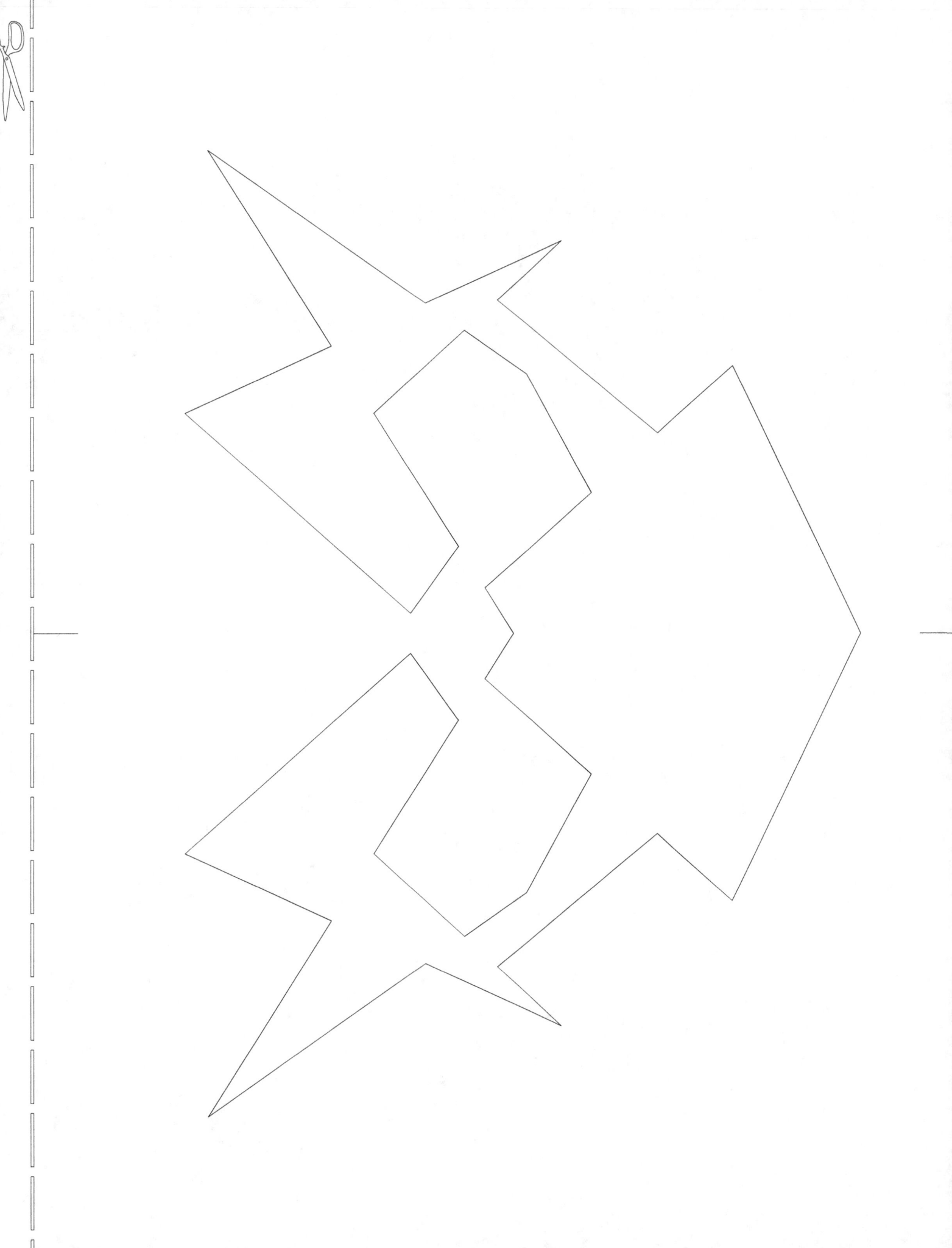

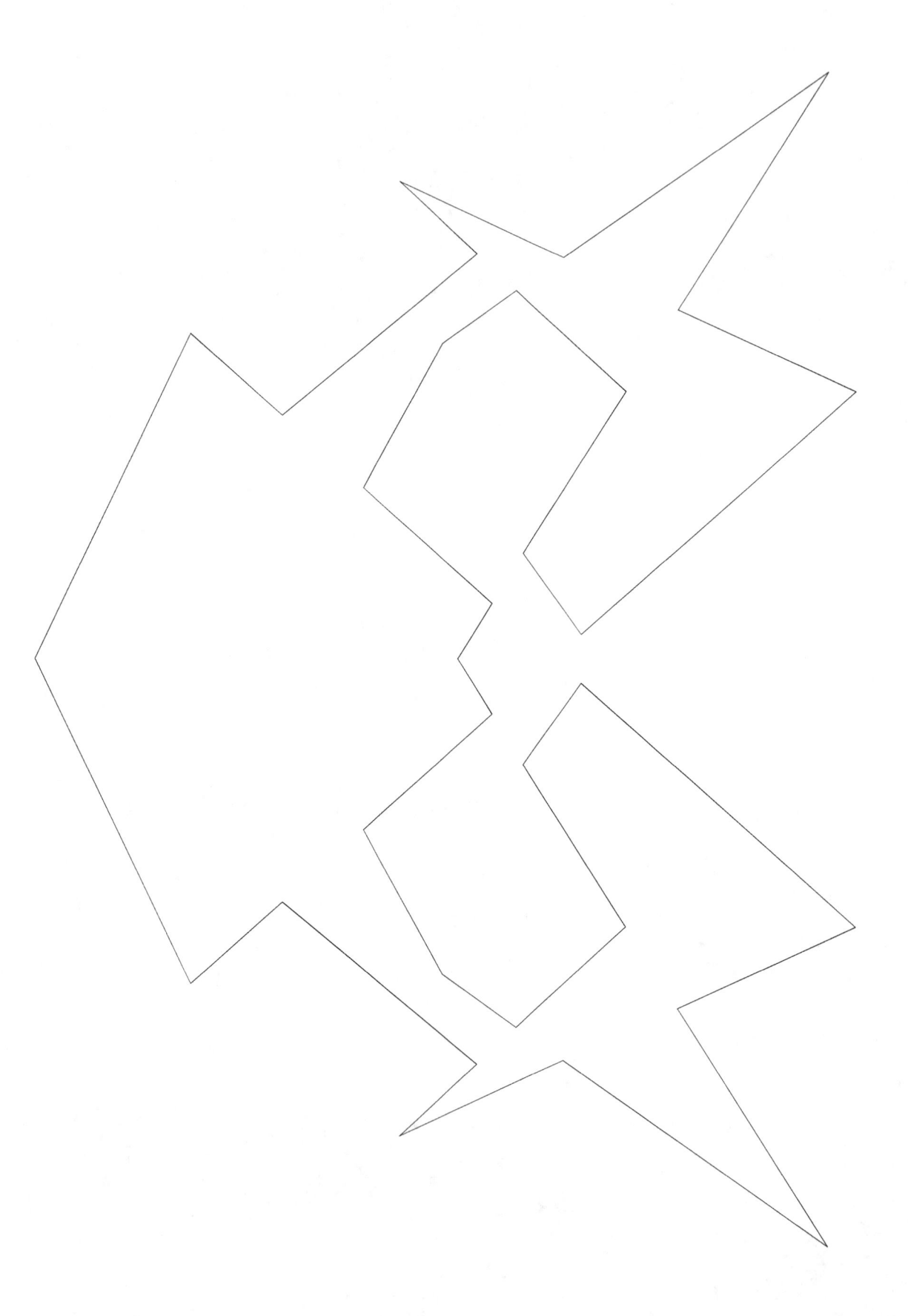

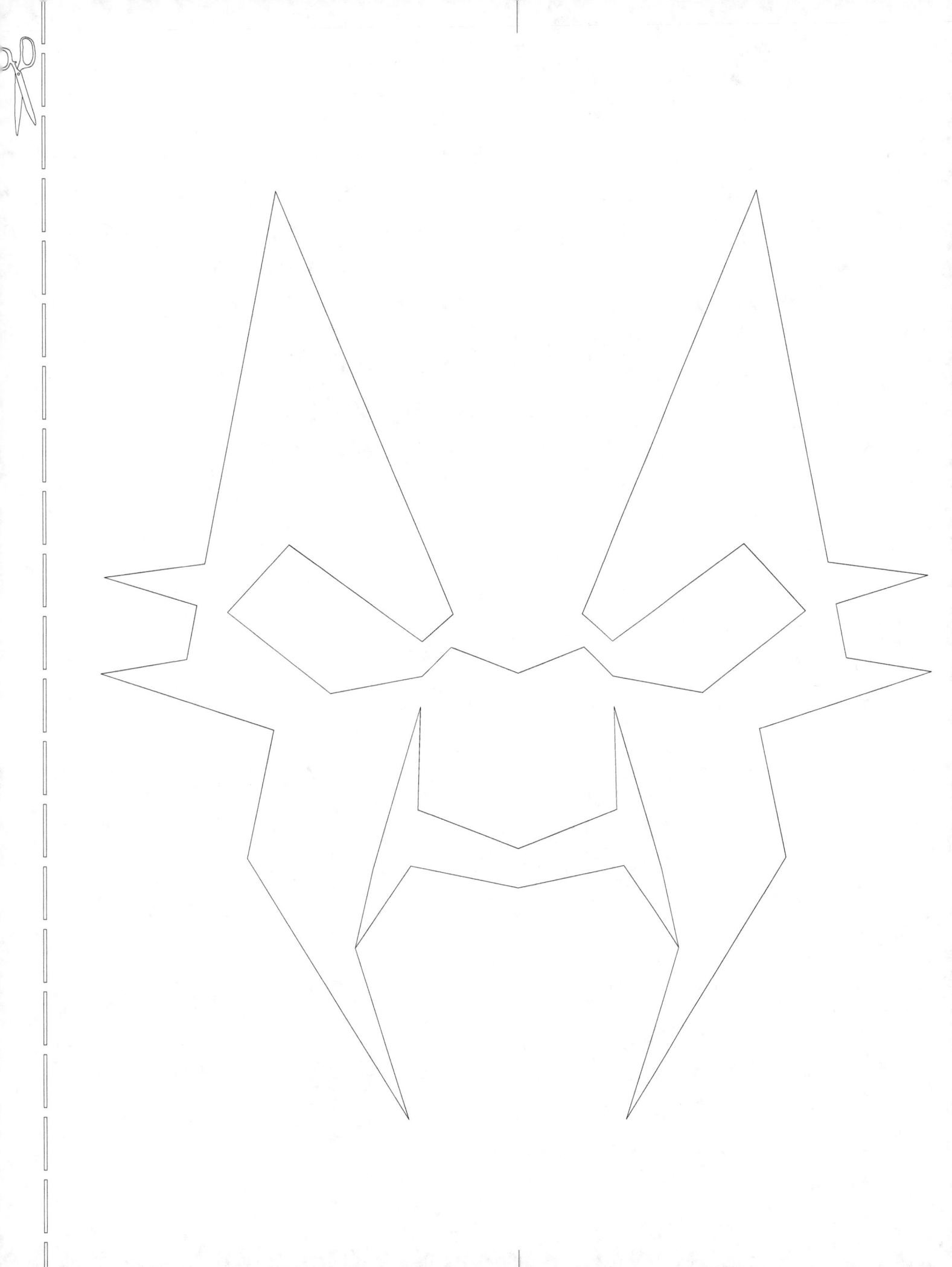

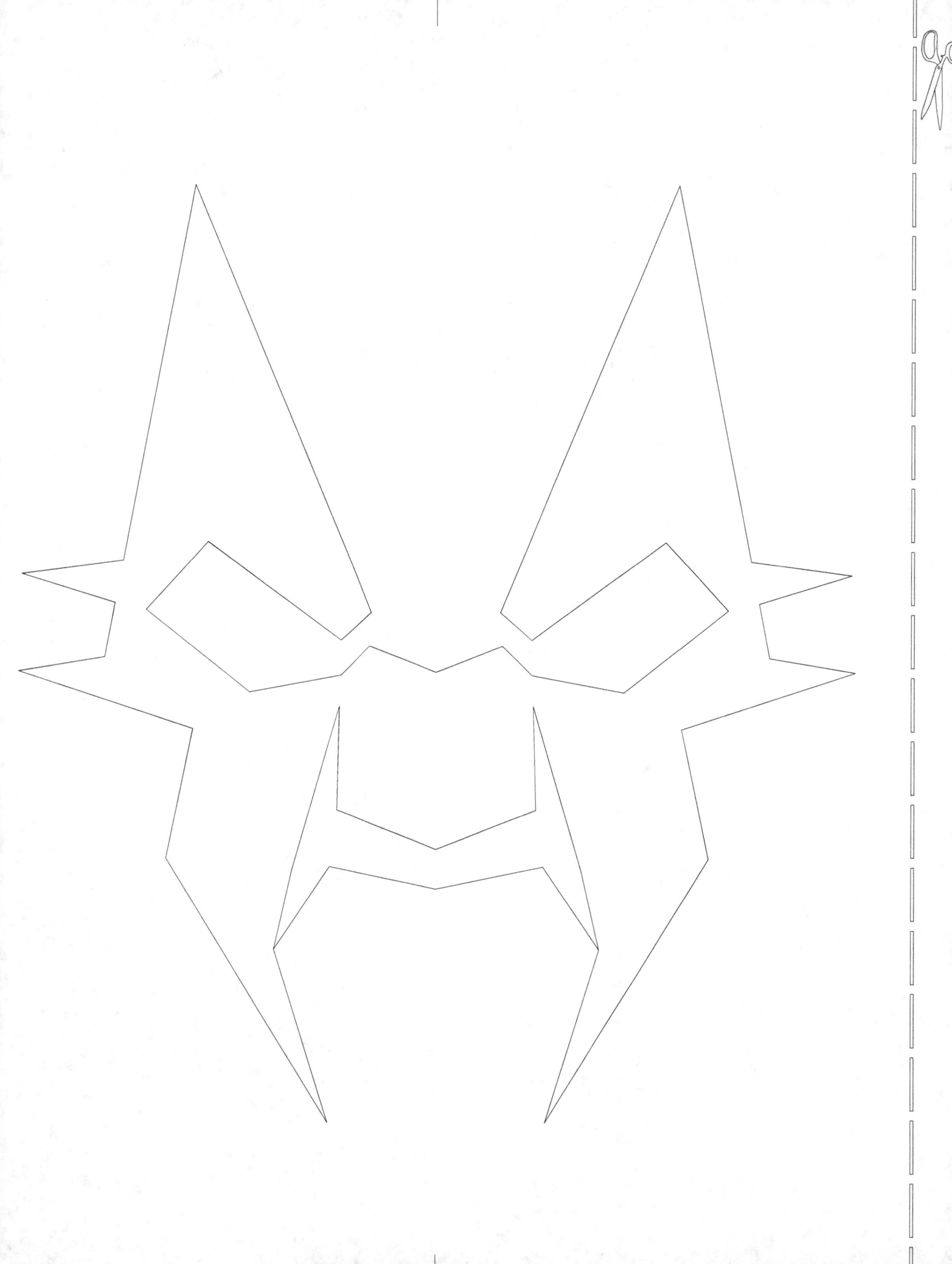

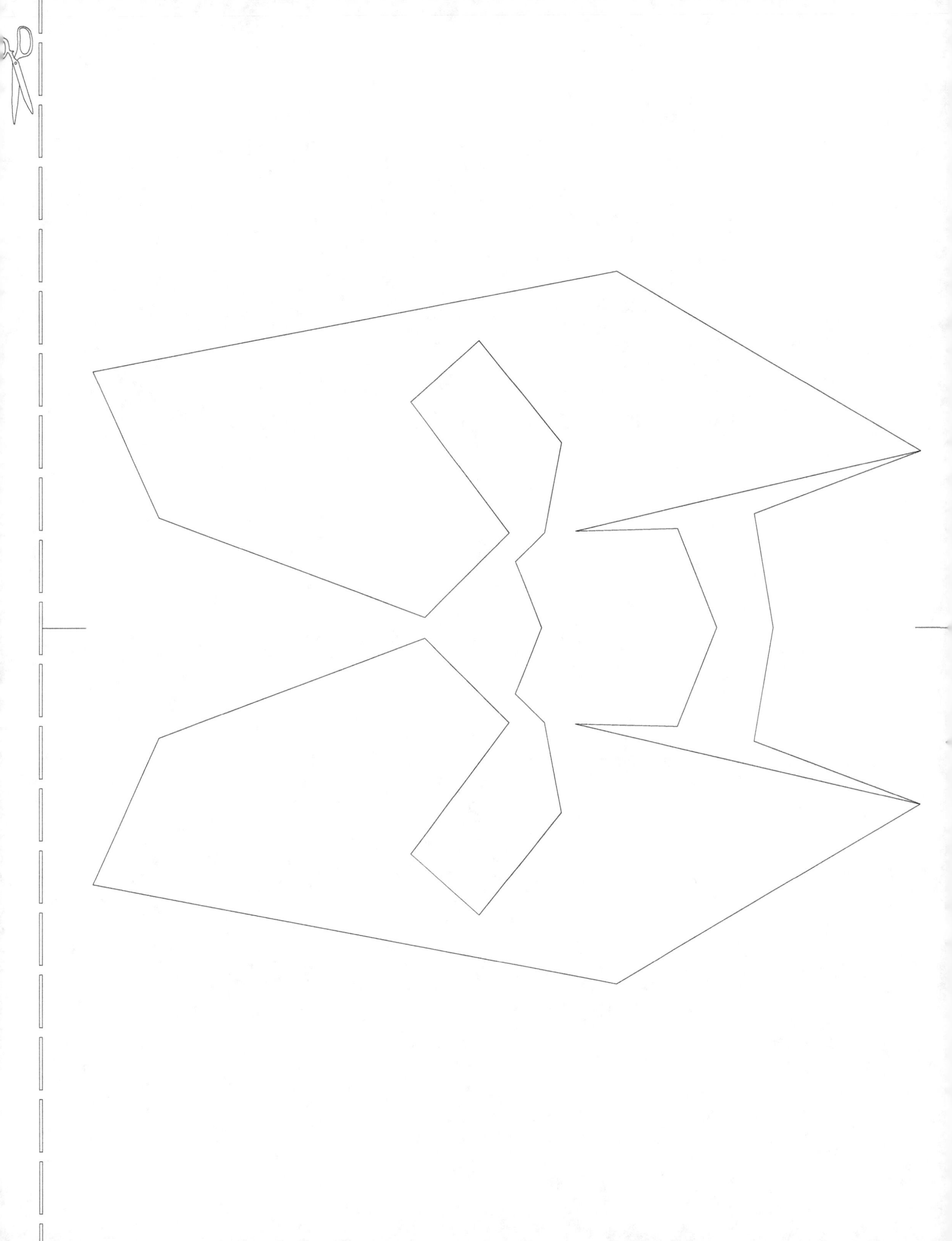

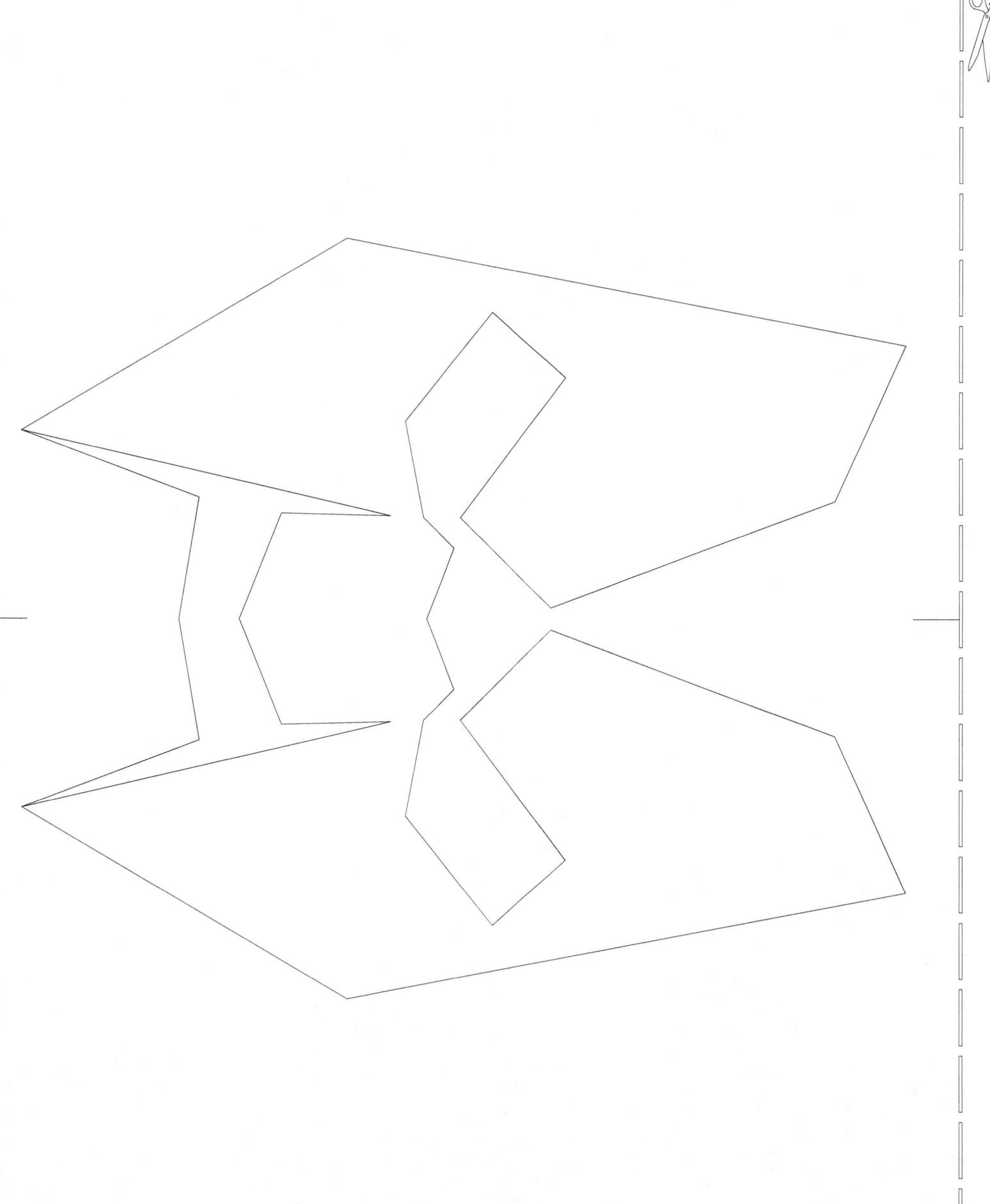

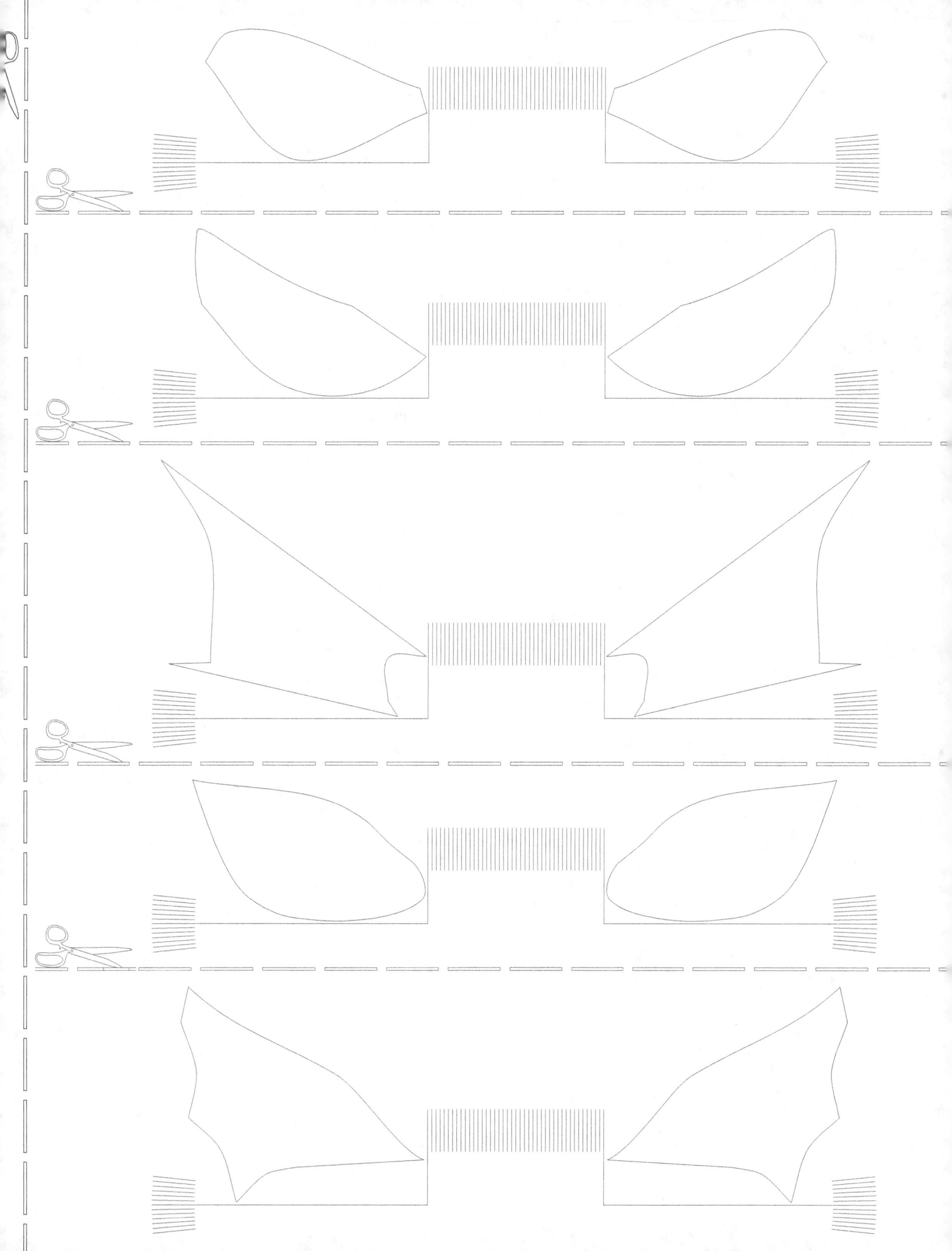

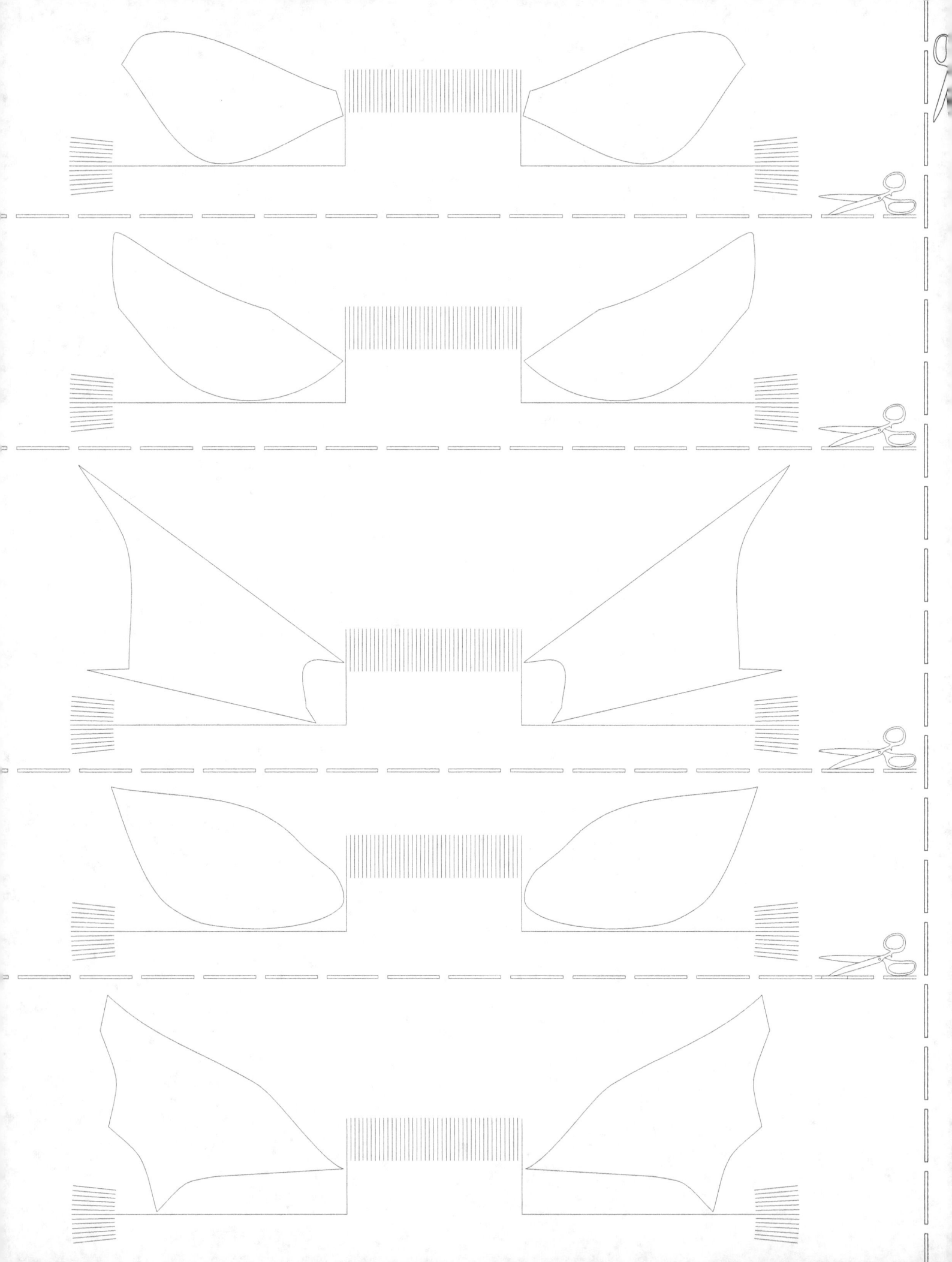

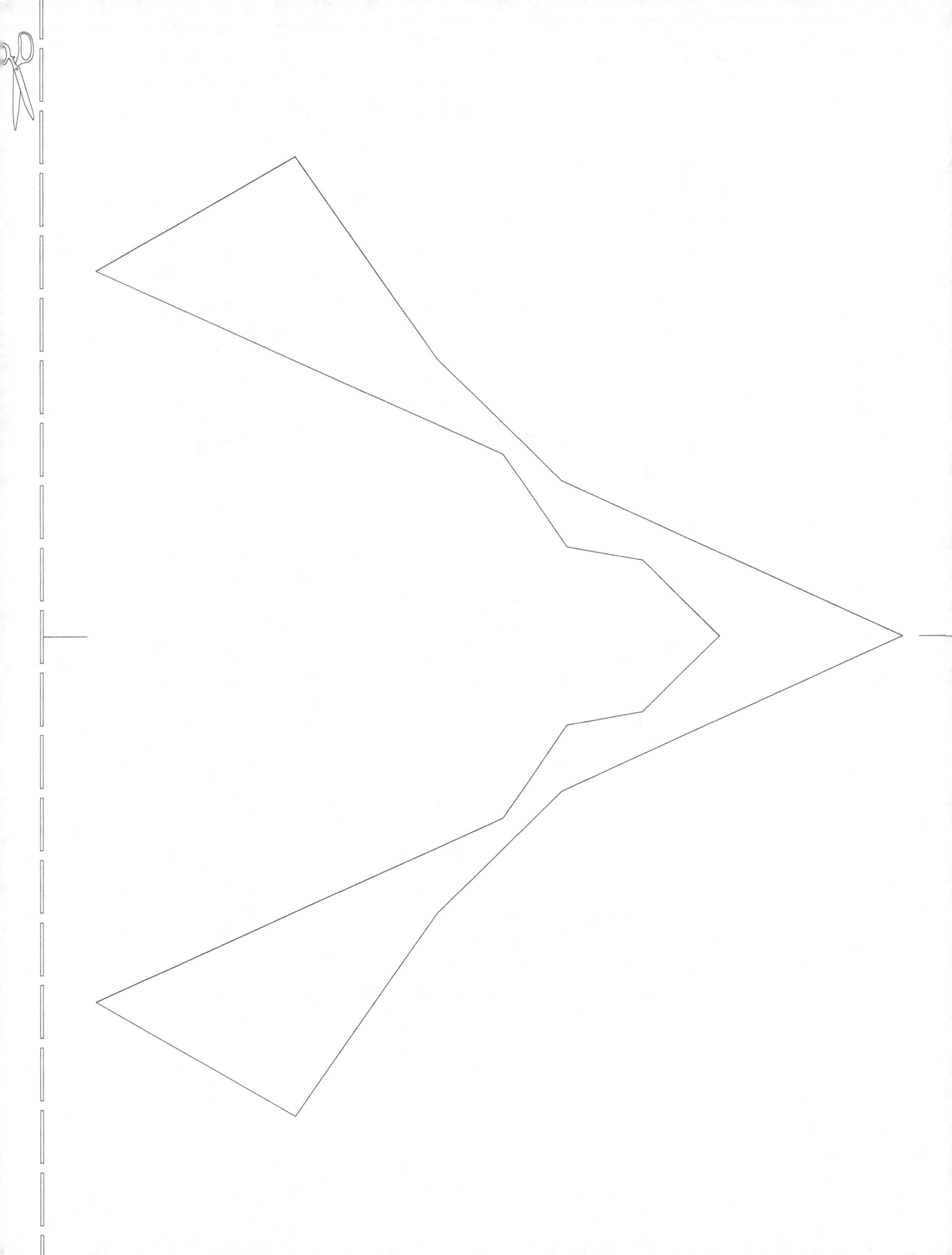

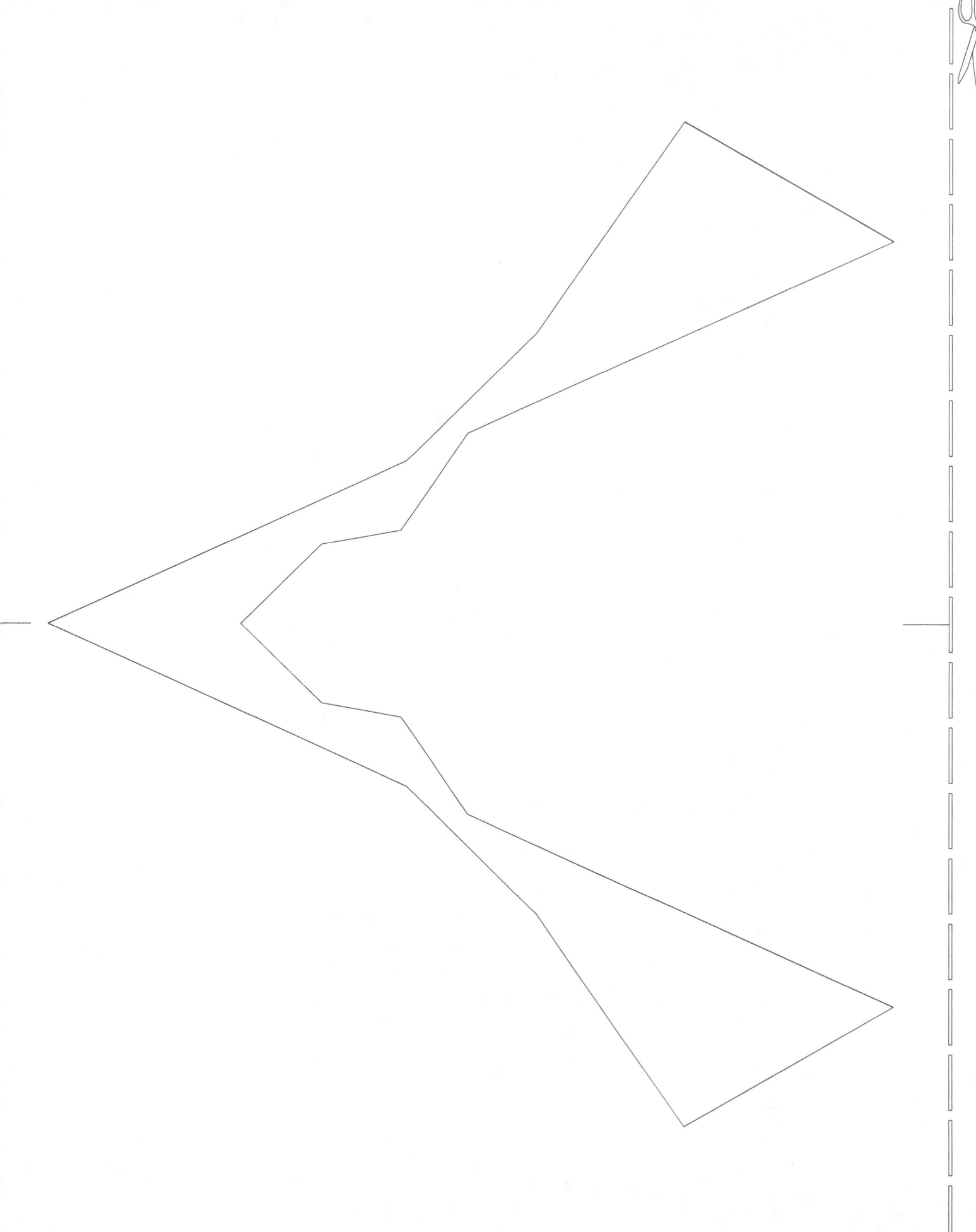

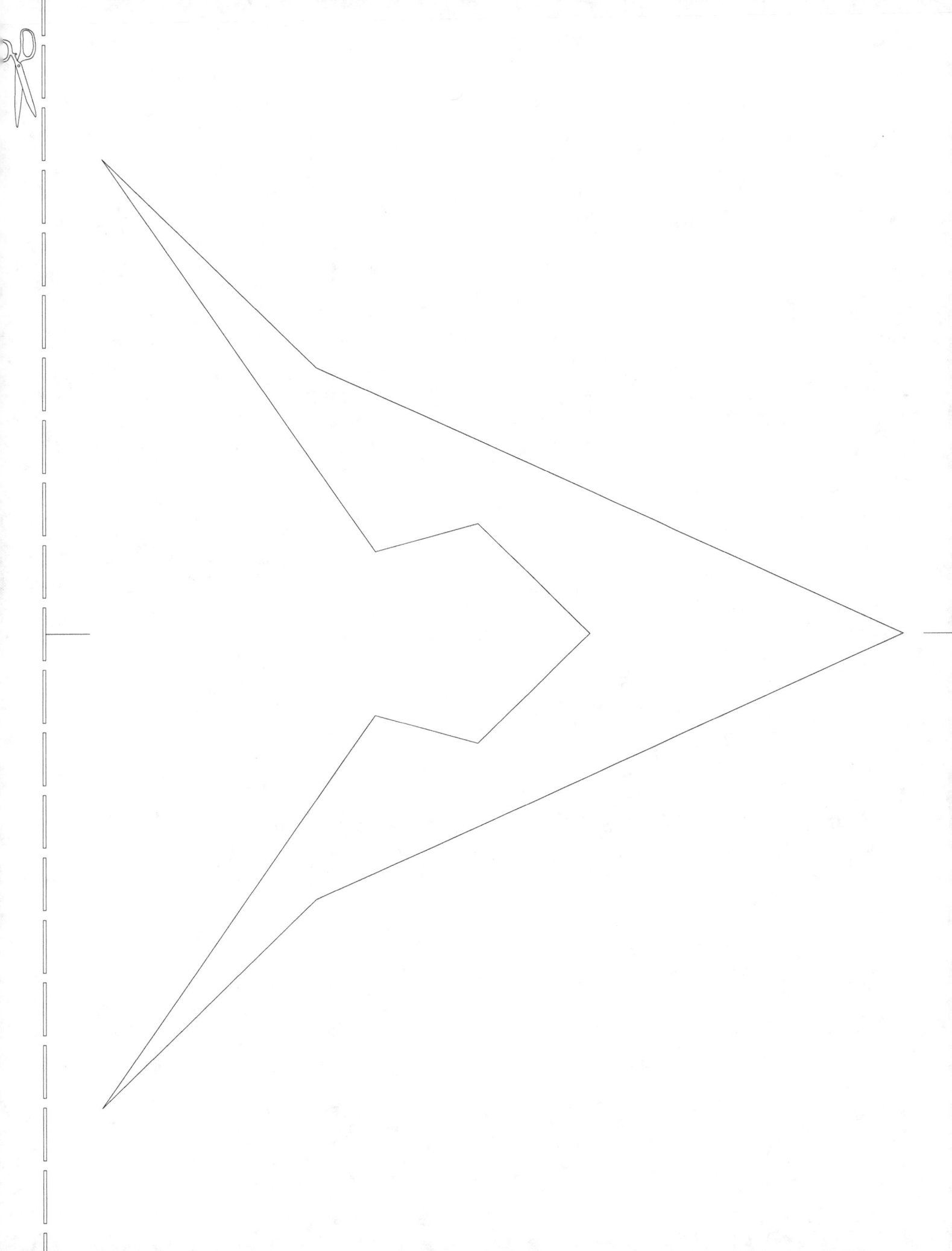

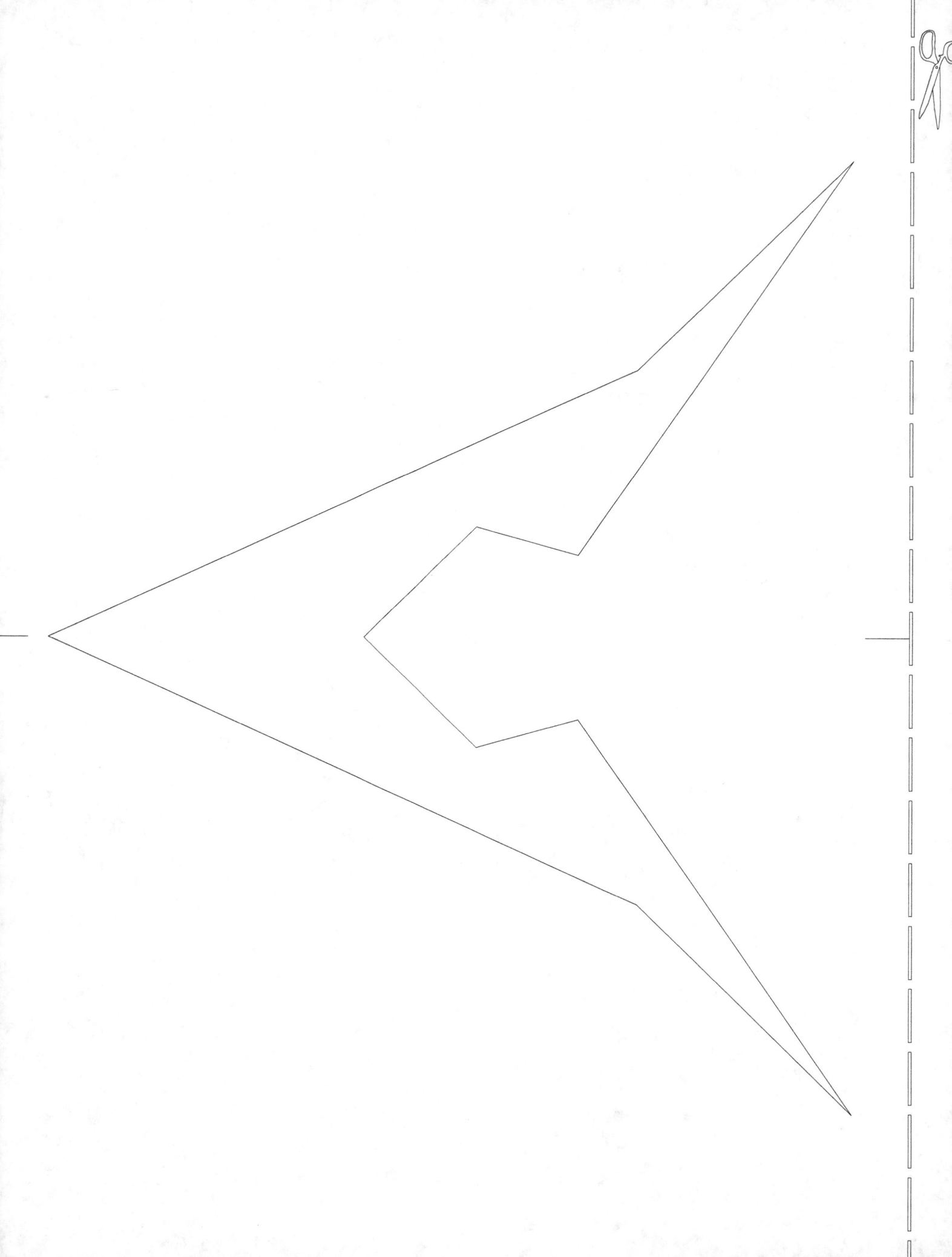

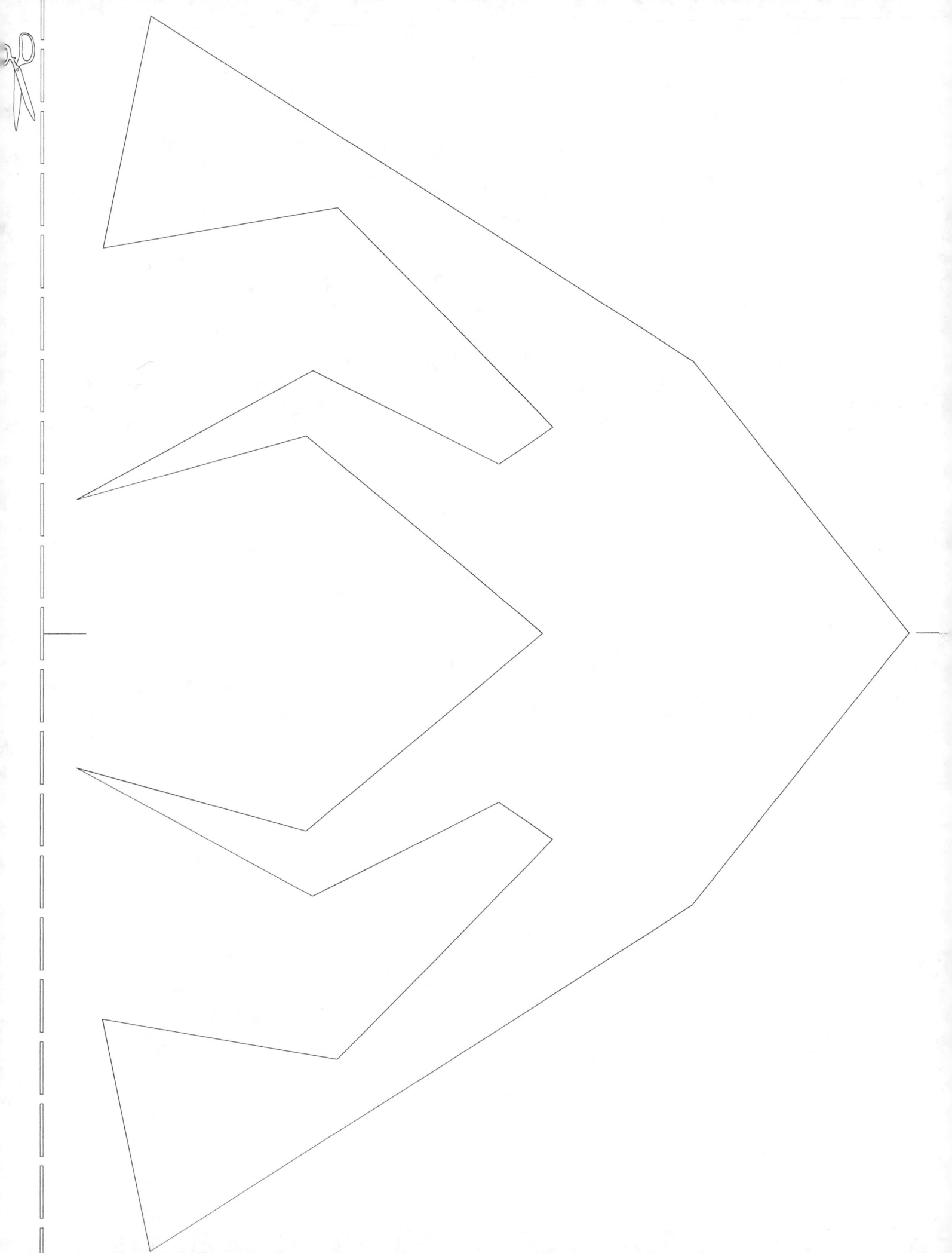

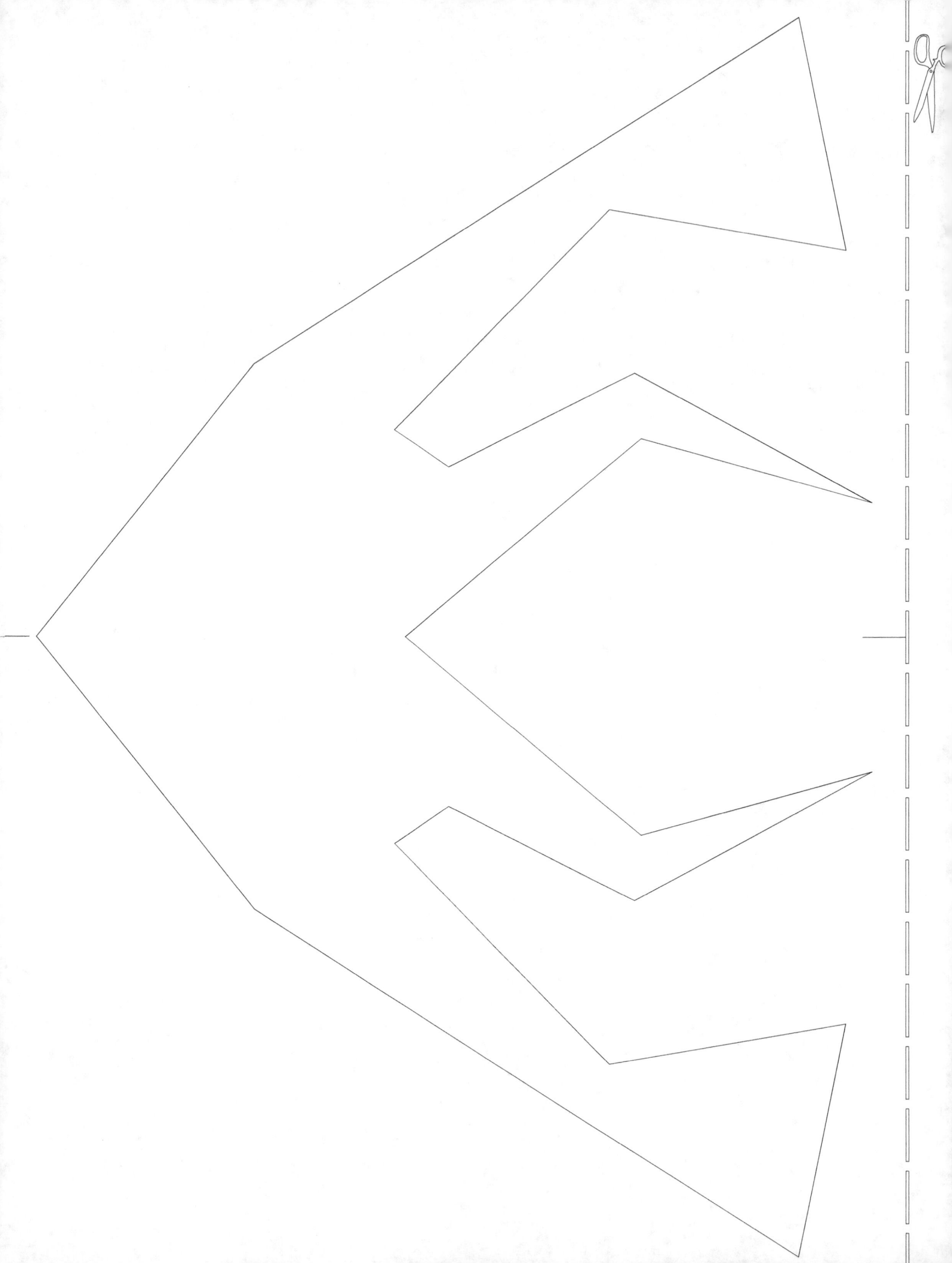

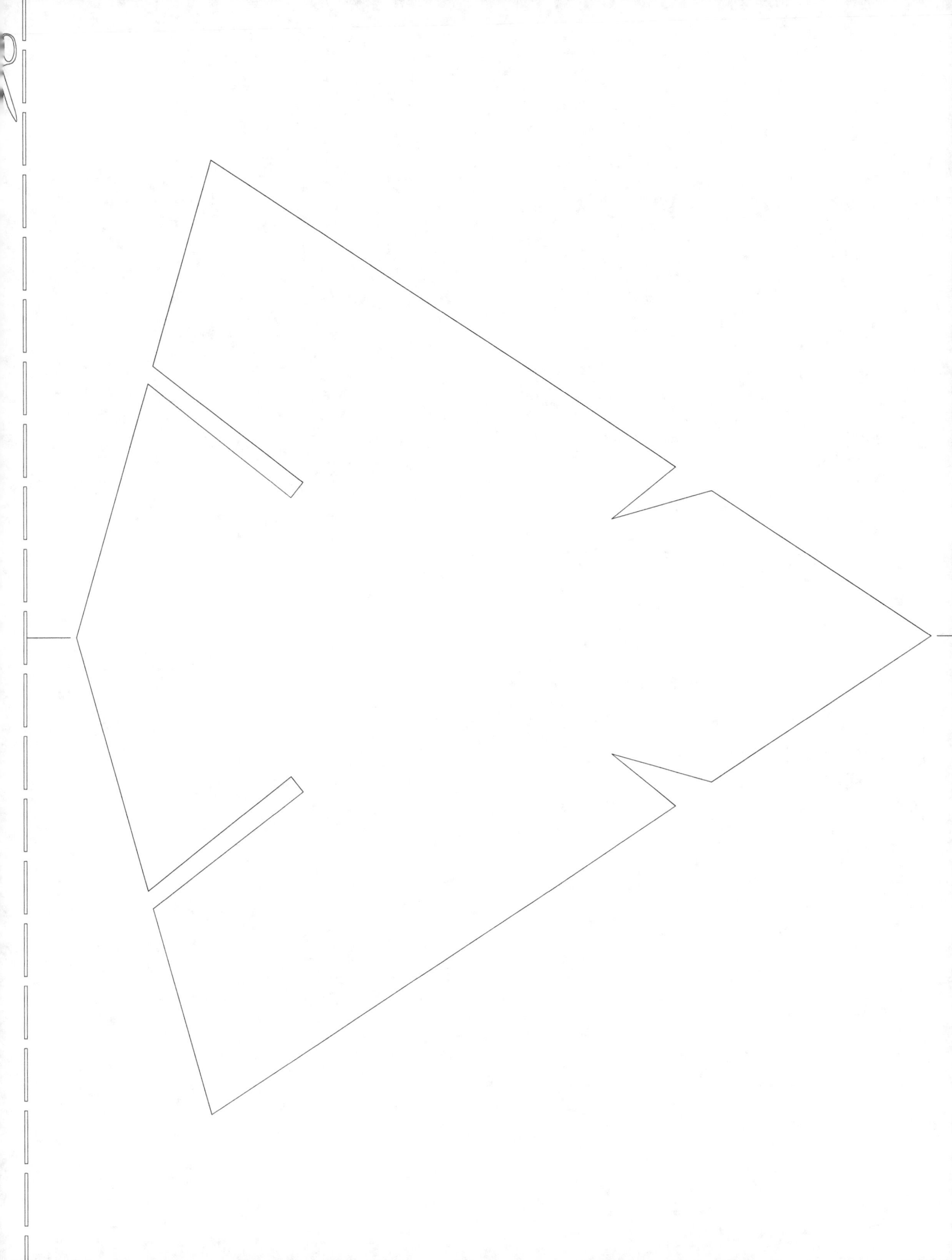

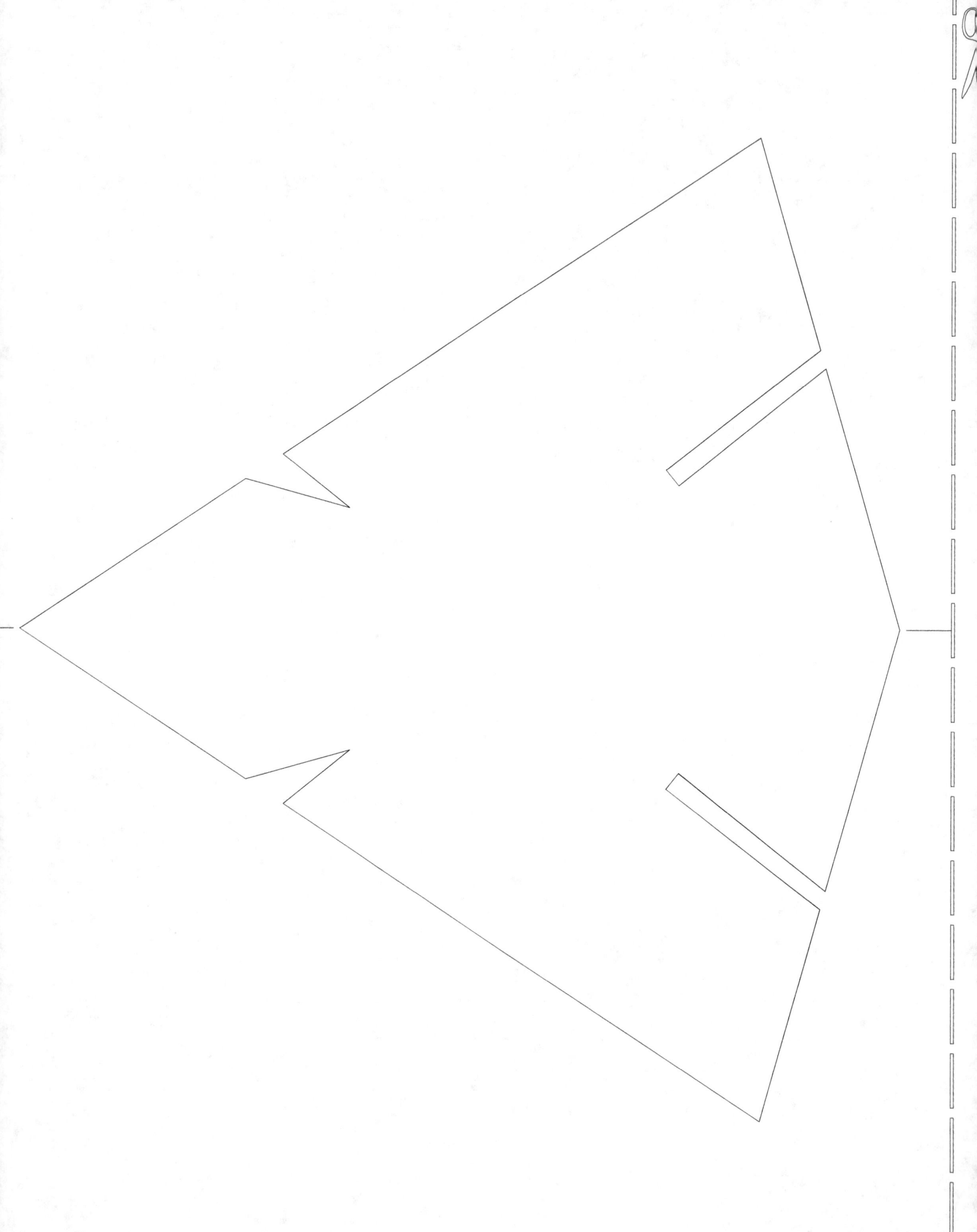

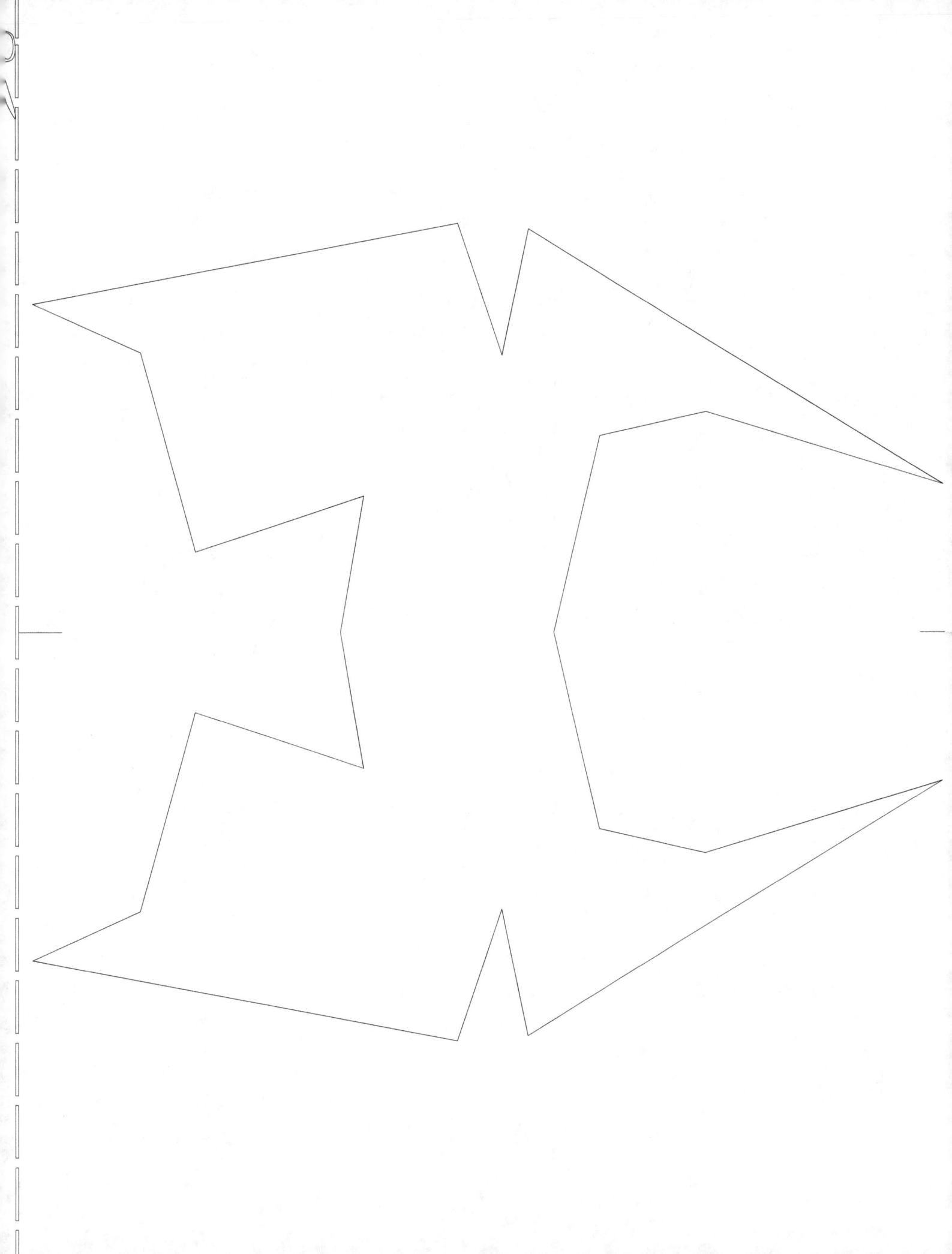

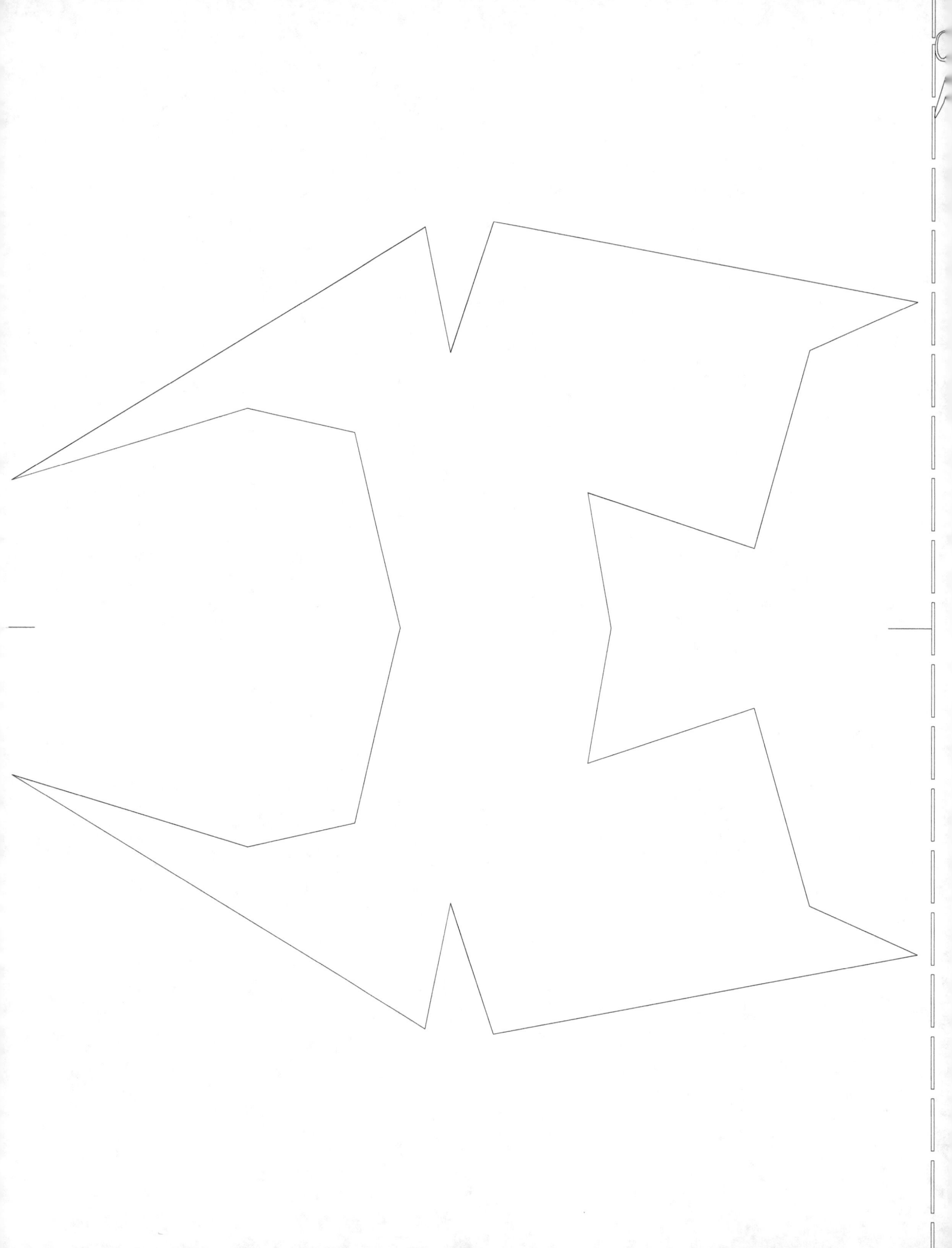

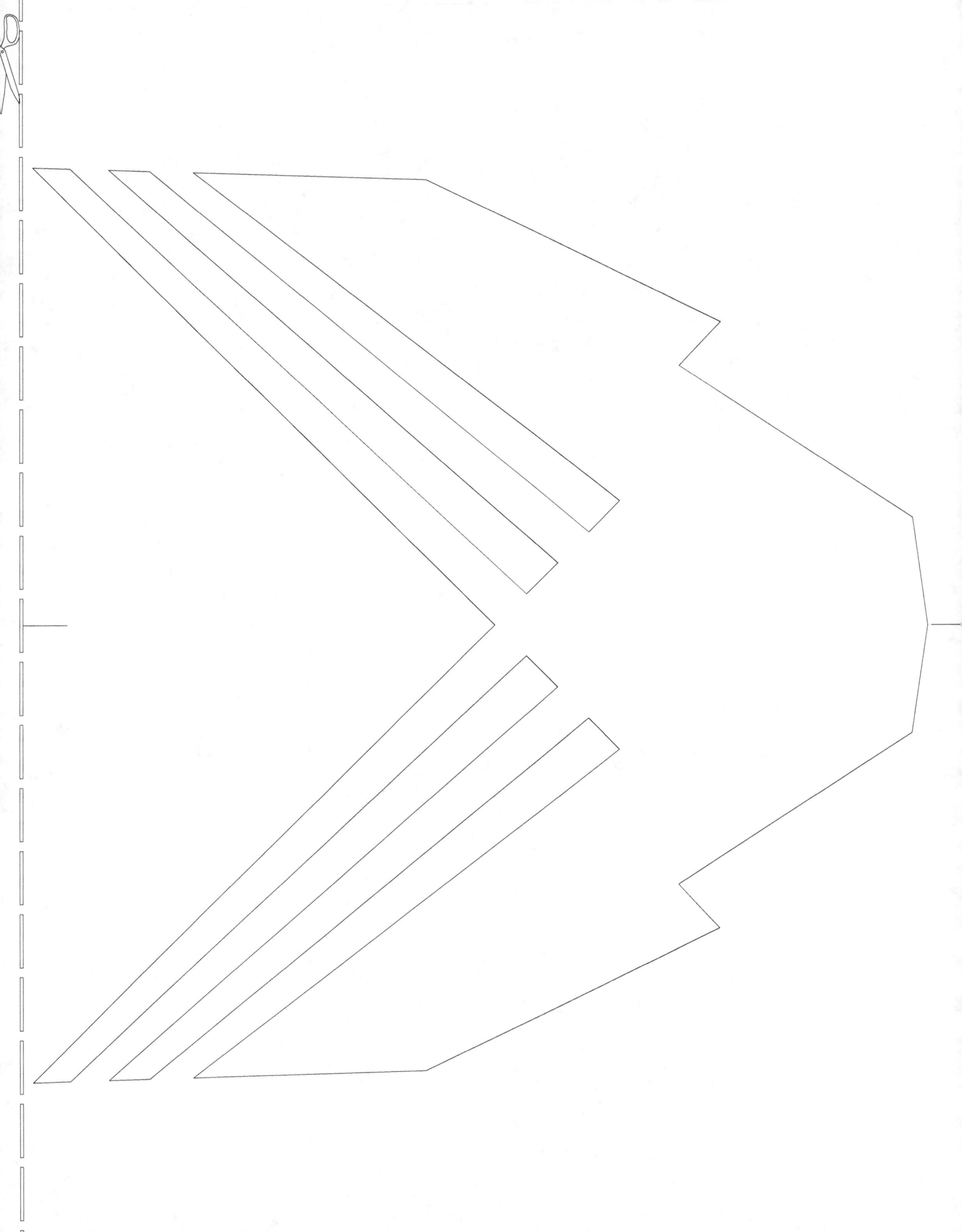

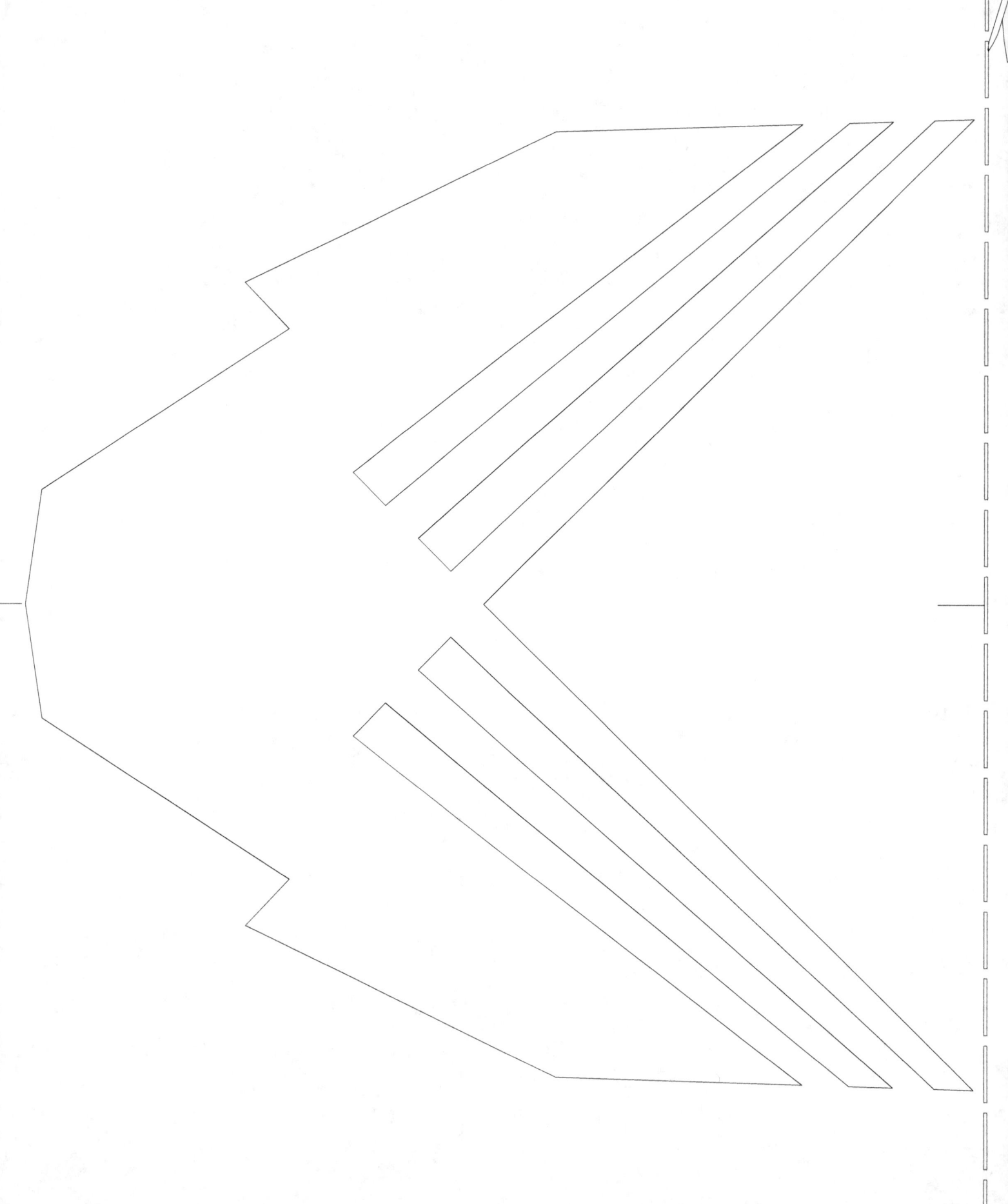

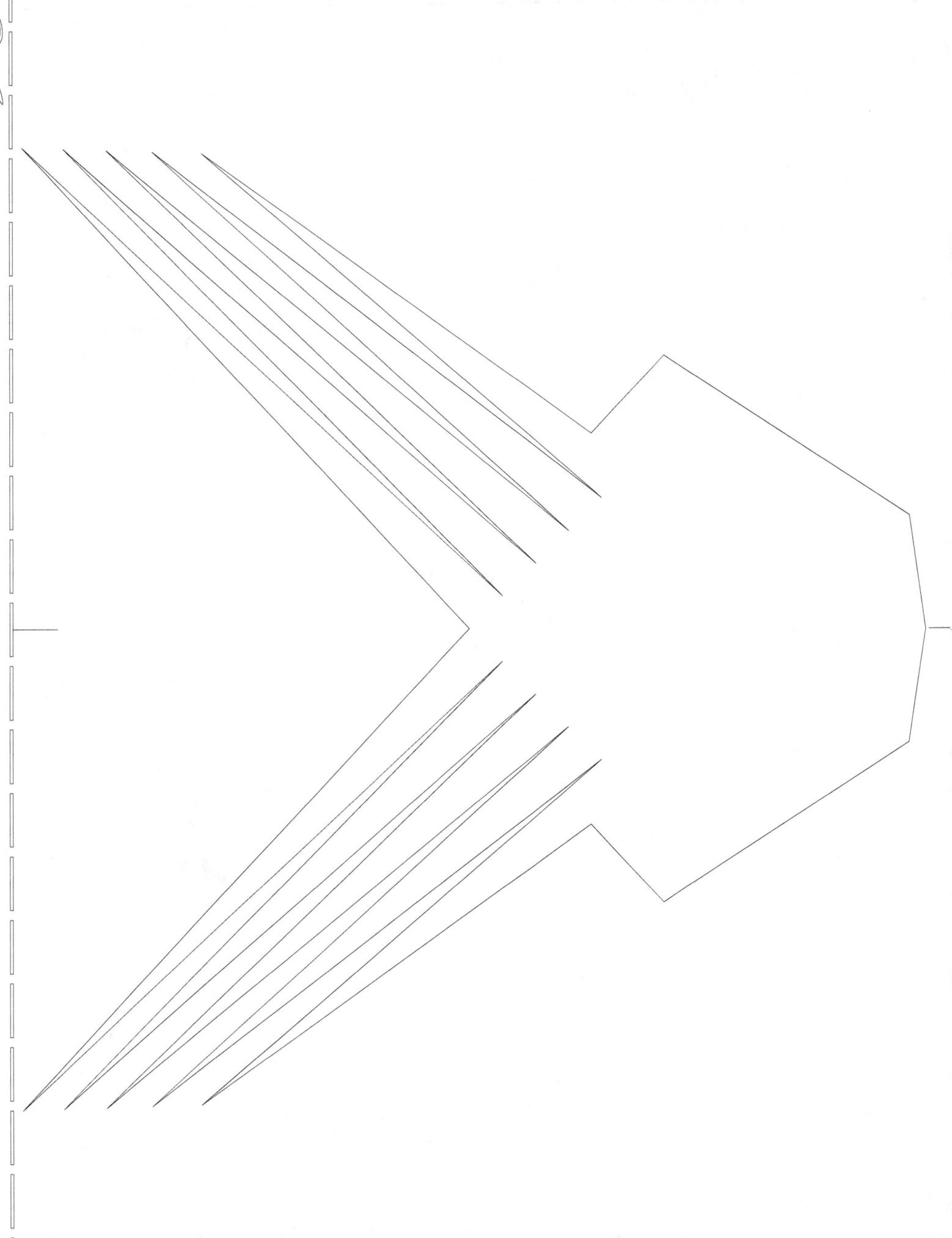

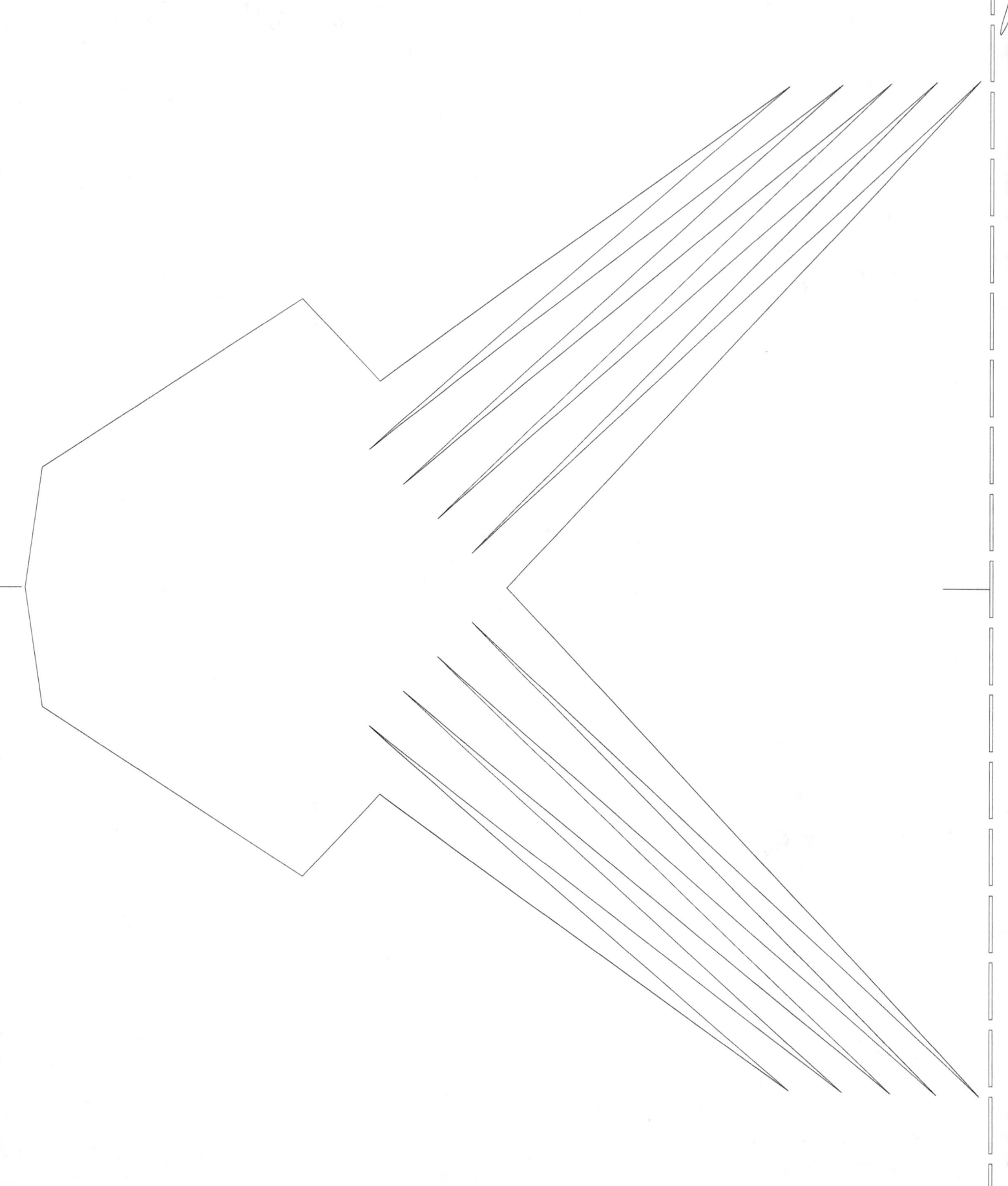

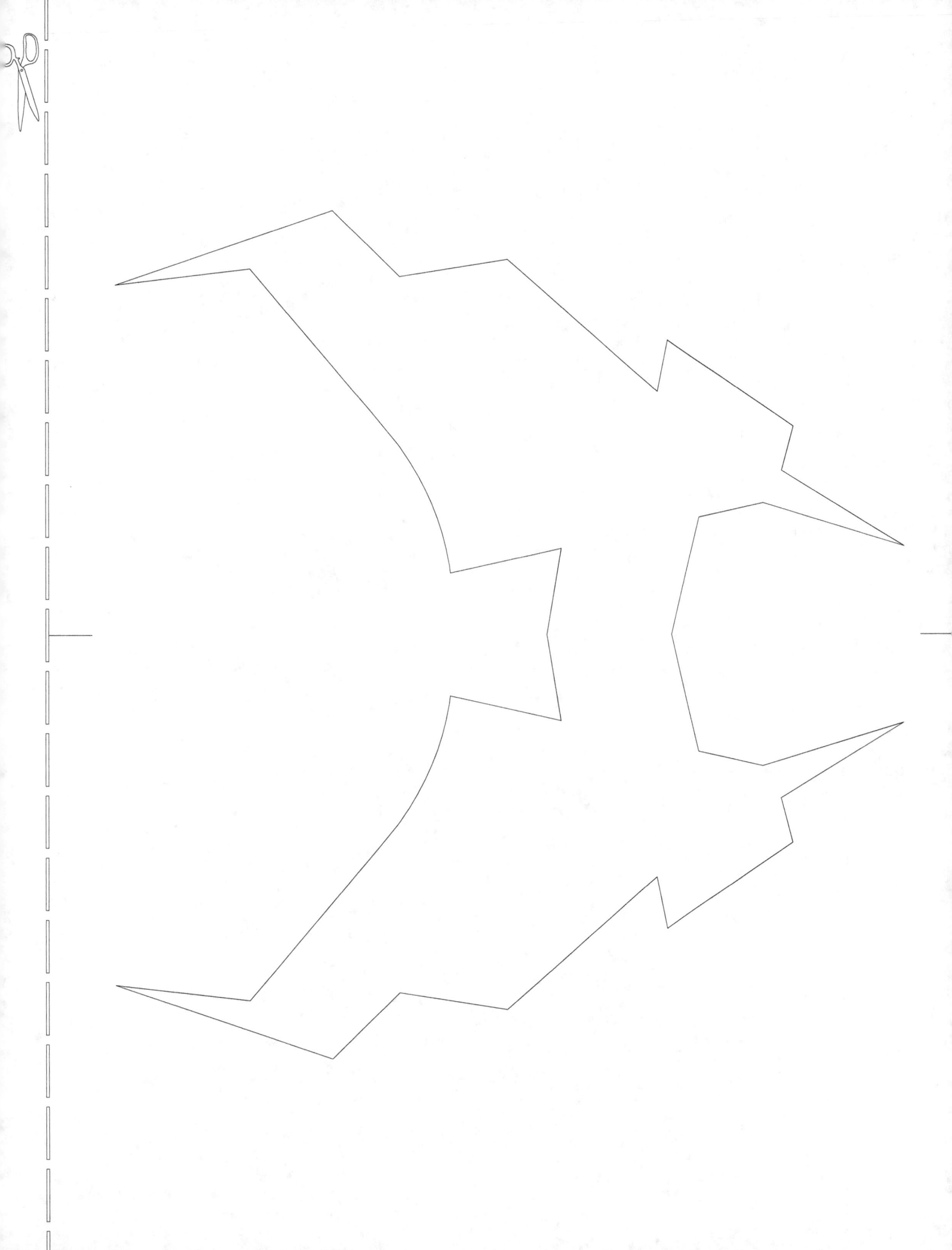

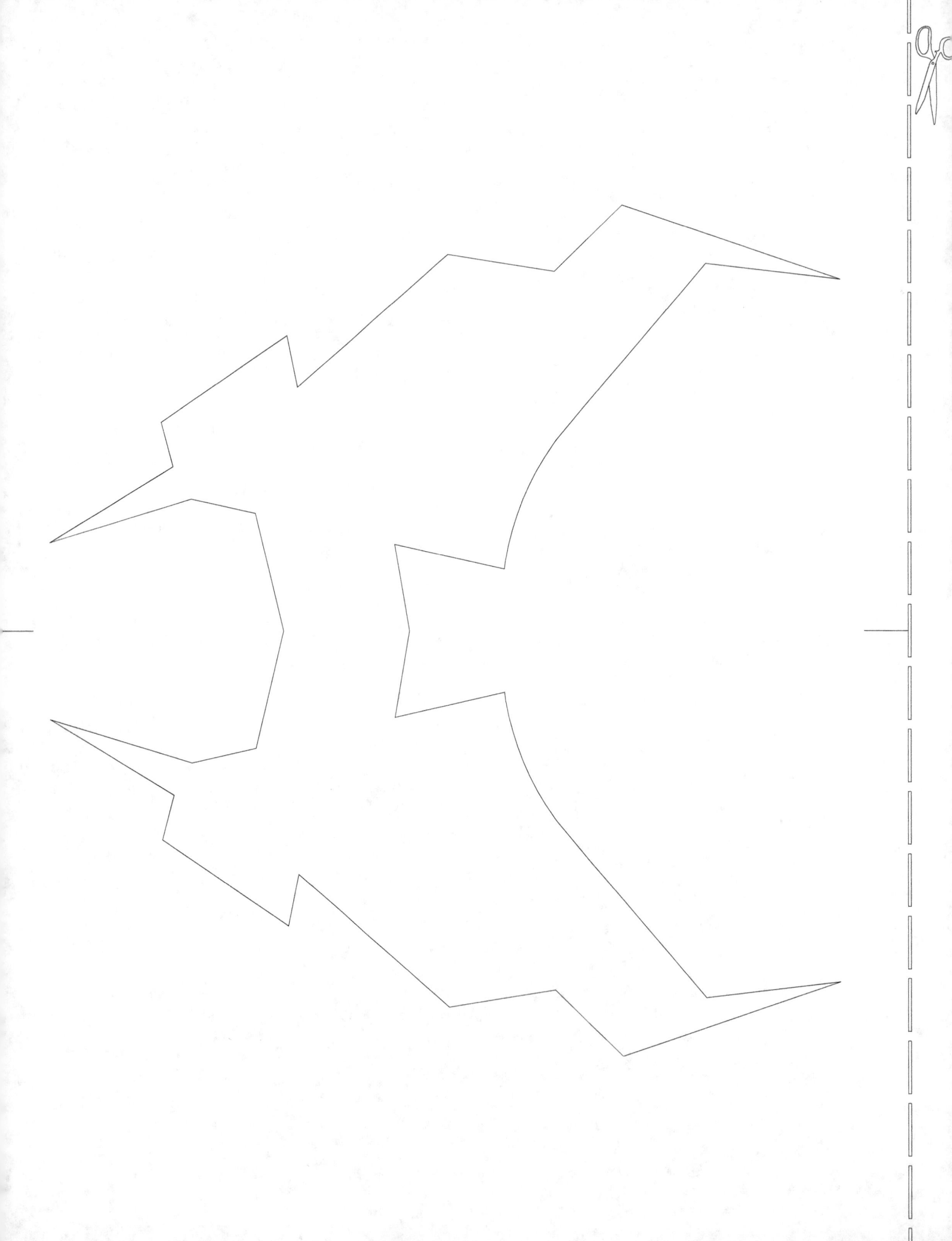

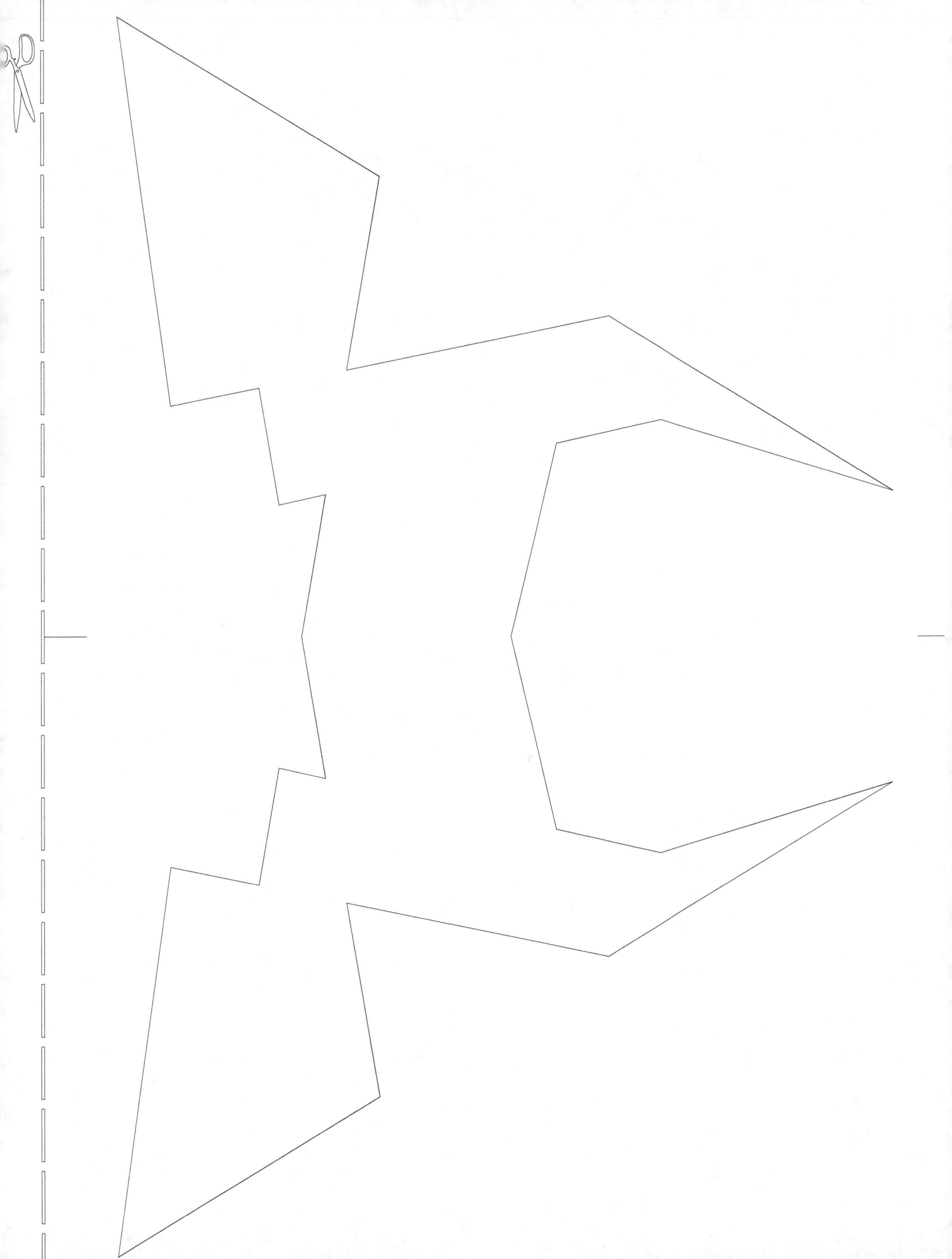

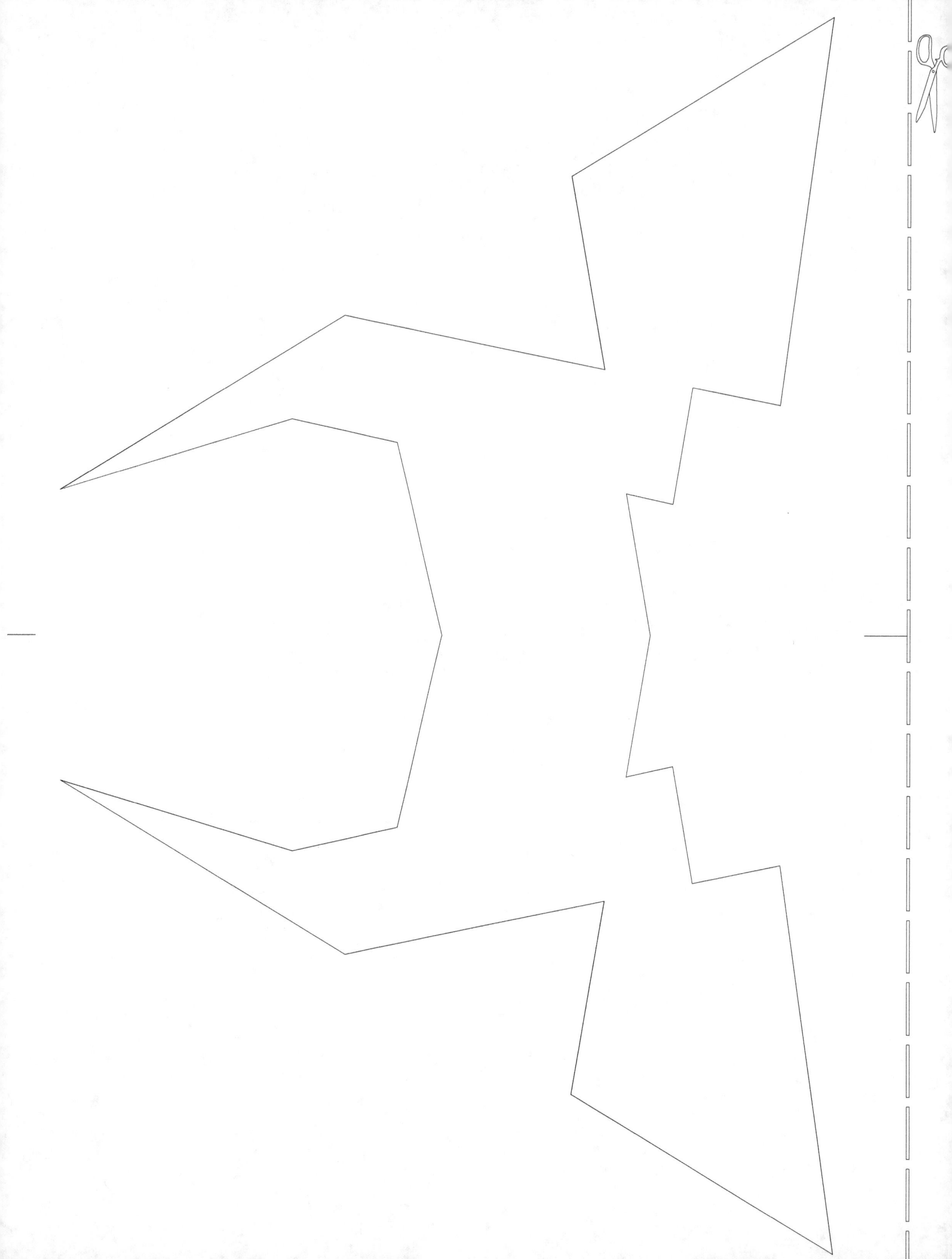